YESHIVATH BETH MOSHE OF SCRANTON
*is proud of its many contributions to
Torah scholarship. Since its beginning
in 1965, the Scranton Yeshiva has elevated the
calibre of Torah education through its high school,
beis medrash and Kollel-Graduate Program.*

*Our alumni rank among the leading
educators and lay leaders in America.*

*Over the years, dissemination of valuable,
informative and spiritually uplifting Jewish literature
has become a tradition at Beth Moshe.
It is in this tradition that we present with pride
this current volume.*

RAMBAM
Maimonides' Introduction to the Mishnah

Translated and Annotated by
AVRAHAM YAAKOV FINKEL

YESHIVATH BETH MOSHE
SCRANTON, PA.

Copyright © 1993
Yeshivath Beth Moshe
930 Hickory Street, Scranton, PA 18505 (717) 346-1747

First Edition

All rights reserved. No part of this publication may be reproduced in any form without written permission from the copyright holders, except for purposes of quotation in a review printed in a newspaper or magazine.

ISBN 0-9626226-2-1

Table Of Contents

Preface	VII
The Written and the Oral Torah	1
The Power of Prophecy	6
The Transmission of the Oral Torah	24
Categories of the Oral Torah	27
Dissenting Opinions	40
The Structure of the Mishnah	42
Expounding the Mishnah	66
Following the Completion of the Talmud	84
Discussion About the Commentary on the Mishnah	87
Appendix	91
Glossary	113

Translator's Preface

Rabbeinu Moshe ben Maimon, better known as the Rambam (Maimonides) (1135-1204), is considered one of the greatest codifiers and philosophers in Jewish history. This Torah giant is the author of many works, including the monumental Mishneh Torah, a seminal, comprehensive Code of Jewish law, and Moreh Nevuchim, "Guide for the Perplexed," one of the greatest works on Jewish philosophy ever written.

Born in 1135 in Cordova, Spain, the Rambam's early life was marred by persecution, flight and restless wanderings. It was during these turbulent times that the Rambam, at the age of twenty-three, wrote the Commentary on the Mishnah.

His introduction to this work—translated in this volume—is in itself a document of great importance, since it contains a comprehensive formulation of the process by which the Oral Law was transmitted, from Moshe until Rabbi Yehudah HaNasi, the compiler of the Mishnah.

The significance of this discourse lies in the fact that the Rambam conveys the proper outlook needed for the study of the Mishnah. He emphasizes that Halachah is not determined by prophetic pronouncements but by analysis of the law by the Rabbis according to a set of prescribed rules.

This leads into a detailed discussion of prophecy, and the ways of distinguishing between a true and a false prophet.

The Rambam goes on to classify the Oral Law, clearly defining *Halachos leMoshe miSinai* (Laws received by Moses in Sinai), enactments (*takkanos*) and preventive measures (*gezeiros*).

He then proceeds to give an outline of the Mishnah itself, describing the six Orders (*Sedarim*) and the topics discussed in the various tractates (*masechtos*). He goes into greater detail with tractate *Avos* (Ethics of the Fathers), focusing on the role of a judge.

We are given an explanation of the origin of halachic disagreements and how these controversies led to the writing of the Talmud where these debates are recorded.

There follows a detailed overview of the nature of Aggadic *derashos* on which the Rambam explains that these seemingly bizarre tales must be seen as allegories concealing profound concepts that cannot be spelled out in simple language. This leads into a very enlightening philosophical discussion about the purpose of the creation of man, and the ideals man should pursue.

The Rambam then lists all the Orders and Tractates of the Talmud and concludes by describing his purpose in writing the commentary on the Mishnah.

The Introduction to the Mishnah is a work of sheer genius, for it offers in capsule form, a perspective on the contents of the entire Mishnah and the Talmud. More importantly, it fills us with awe and reverence for the towering Sages, the bearers of the torch, who handed the Oral Law to us in its pristine purity, link after link, in an unbroken chain.

The Rambam wrote his work in Arabic, in order to make it accessible to the widest spectrum of the Jews of his time whose native tongue this language was. It was translated into Hebrew by Rabbi Yehudah ben Shlomoh Charizi and can be found in the Vilna edition of *meseches Berachos*, in the commentary section, page 105.

In translating the Introduction I have attempted to make the difficult text accessible to a wide range of readers by presenting it in an informal, colloquial English, following the Rambam's example who wrote in Arabic in order to reach the largest possible readership.

I kept the translation as literal as possible. Where the literal translation made it difficult to comprehend, I modified it slightly as the Rambam himself instructed to the translators of his works. Additions to the text and the translation of words that are necessary to understand the text, are placed in brackets. The translation of other words can be found in the glossary.

Rabbi Zvi Lampel's scholarly work "The Introduction to the Talmud", published by Judaica Press, was an invaluable aid to this project. I would like to thank Mr. J. Goldman of Judaica Press for his assistance to the Yeshiva in the publication of this translation.

It is my hope that this volume will whet the readers' appetite for studying the Mishnah, *lilmod ulelameid, lishmor velaasos*—to learn, to teach, and to do.

The Written and the Oral Torah

Every *mitzvah* the Holy One, Blessed is He, gave to *Moshe Rabbeinu*, was given to him together with its explanation. Hashem would tell Moshe a verse of the Torah, and then He would give to him its explanation, its underlying principles and all the cases to which the verse applies.

Moshe, in person, taught each verse of the Torah to the assembly of the *B'nei Yisrael* in the presence of Aharon and the Elders.[1]

Afterwards, the people reviewed with one another what they had heard from Moshe, and wrote down the verse on scrolls. Supervisors would visit the people to teach and review the verse until everyone knew it

---

1. The Talmud relates that Moshe taught the Torah to *B'nei Yisrael* in the following manner:

    Moshe would enter his tent, and Aharon would be the first to follow. Moshe would tell Aharon the verse once and teach him its explanation. Aharon would then position himself on Moshe's right side, after which Aharon's sons, Elazar and Isamar, entered. Moshe would repeat to them what he had told Aharon, whereupon one son would take a seat on Moshe's right, and the other on Aharon's left. Next, the seventy elders would enter, and Moshe would repeat to them the instruction he had taught to Aharon and his sons.

accurately and was well-versed in it. They then taught the people the explanation of the G-d-given mitzvah in all its many details. Thus, the wording of the mitzvah would be recorded in writing, while its oral tradition would be learned by heart.

This fact [that the written verse was given with its oral explanation] is discussed by our Rabbis in a *Baraisa* (*Sifra, Vayikra* 25:1):

It is written, *"Hashem spoke to Moshe on Mount Sinai . . ."* (*Vayikra 25:1*). [This verse introduces a detailed discussion of the laws of sh'mittah—the Sabbatical year.] To what purpose does the verse mention Mount Sinai in connection with *sh'mittah*? After all, we know full well that **all** the laws of the Torah were given on Sinai.—Mount Sinai is mentioned here to tell you: Just as the details and particulars of the laws of sh'mittah are written openly in the Torah and were obviously given at Sinai, so too the details of the other mitzvos [although not mentioned in the written Torah], were also given at Sinai.

For example, the Holy One, Blessed is He, told Moshe the verse, *"You must live in sukkos for seven days"*

Then the people at large, all those seeking Hashem, would come, and Moshe would present the verse to them, so that they would hear it entirely from his own lips.

As a result, Aharon heard each verse from Moshe's lips four times, his sons, three times, the elders, twice, and the rest of the people heard it once.

Moshe would then withdraw, and Aharon would explain to the assembled crowd the verse which he had heard from Moshe four times. Elazar and Isamar would then restate the verse to the people, after which the elders taught the same verse to the entire assemblage once more.

Consequently, B'nei Yisrael heard the verse four times: once from Moshe, once from Aharon, a third time from his sons, and a fourth time from the elders. *(Eiruvin 54b)*

(*Vayikra* 23:42). Afterwards Hashem let Moshe know that this mitzvah needs to be fulfilled by all males but not by females, (*Sukkah* 2.8) that the sick and travelers are not required to live in a *sukkah*, (*Sukka* 26a) that the roof of the sukkah must be made of something which grows from the ground (thus excluding wool, silk and the like), and may not be made of utensils, even those made from plant material, such as quilts, pillows and clothing (*Sukkah* 1:4). Hashem also let Moshe know that one must eat, drink and sleep in the sukkah during all the seven days of *Sukkos*, and that the interior area of a sukkah may not be less than seven handbreadth square, and that it may not be less than ten handbreadth in height (*Sukkah* 16b). In this way, the mitzvah of sukkah was given to Moshe together with its detailed explanations.

And so it was with all the 613 mitzvos; Moshe received the mitzvos along with their explanations; the mitzvos he received in writing and their explanations, orally.

On the first of *Shevat*, in the fortieth year of the wandering of B'nei Yisrael in the desert, shortly before Moshe Rabbeinu's death, Moshe gathered the B'nei Yisrael and told them, "The time of my death is approaching. Whoever has heard a *halachah* but forgot it, come and ask me, and I will explain it to you. Whoever is in doubt about something, tell me about it, and I will clarify it for you," as it says in the Torah, *"In the fortieth year on the first of the eleventh month, Moshe began to explain this Torah, saying"* (Devarim 1:5).

From the first of Sh'vat until the seventh of *Adar* [the day of Moshe's death], the B'nei Yisrael received clarification of the halachos directly from Moshe and studied the explanations. Shortly before his death, Moshe began to write the Torah on scrolls—thirteen parchment Torah scrolls—all containing the full Torah text from the *beis* of *bereishis* [the first letter in the Torah] to the last *lamed* of *le'einei kol Yisrael* [the last letter of the Torah].

He gave one scroll to each of the twelve tribes of Yisrael, instructing them to live according to its laws and to follow its decrees. The thirteenth scroll he gave to the *Levi'im*, telling them, *"Take this Torah scroll and place it beside the ark of the covenant of Hashem your G-d, leaving it there as a witness"* (*Devarim* 31:26).

After that, he climbed *Mount Nevo* on the seventh of Adar at noon, as has been calculated by traditional sources.(*Megillah* 13b)

To us it seems as though Moshe had died, because he is no longer with us and we miss him; but in reality, he lives on, at a loftier level of existence, a higher plane to which he was elevated. The Sages had this in mind when they said, "Moshe Rabbeinu did not die, but rose on high and now serves Hashem in heaven."(*Sotah* 13a) However, a thorough discussion of this subject would take up too much space, and this is not the place for it.

After Moshe died, *Yehoshua* and the Sages of his time studied and researched the explanations they received from Moshe. No question or dispute arose regarding any matter that Yehoshua or any of the elders had explicitly heard from Moshe himself. However, related cases, for which Moshe had not given specific instruction, were solved by applying the Thirteen Rules by means of which the Torah is expounded—rules that were given on Sinai.

Some of the laws derived this way were undisputed and were unanimously agreed upon. Other laws gave rise to controversy. Depending on the precedent to which he compared the case at hand, one Sage would make a statement based on his logical reasoning insisting that he was right, while another Sage would just as vehemently insist that his rationale was right. When such disputes occurred among authorities they would follow the majority opinion, as it is stated, *"[A case] must be decided on the basis of the majority"* (*Shemos* 23:2).

The Power of Prophecy

Prophecy is of no use as a way of explaining the Torah, or as a means of influencing the Thirteen Rules by which subdivisions of mitzvos can be derived. In fact, what Yehoshua and Pinechas [disciples of Moshe, who had access to prophets] did with regard to analysis and explanation of the law is the same as what Ravina and Rav Ashi [who presided over the compilation of the Talmud, when the prophets no longer lived] were to do in their day.

Nevertheless, I assure you by my life, that the extraordinary influence a prophet has on the mitzvos, is one of the fundamental principles on which the Jewish faith rests and is based.

Although I recognize that this is the proper place to explain this fundamental principle, [the role of the prophet], in greater detail, it is impossible to do so without first:

1) sorting out the various claims that can be made to possessing the power of prophecy, and

2) describing the method by which the truth of a prophecy can be verified, since this too, represents a fundamental principle. The vast multitudes of mankind have already erred with regard to this subject,

including a small number of their philosophers. They imagine that a person's power of prophecy is not proven unless he performs a miraculous sign, like one of the signs of *Moshe Rabbeinu*, changing the laws of nature as *Eliyahu* did when he revived the widow's son (*Melachim I 17:22*), or as Elisha did when he performed his famous miracles (*Melachim II* 2:2-9). This is not true. Eliyahu, Elisha and the other prophets did not perform miracles in order to prove the truth of their prophecy. Their reputation as genuine prophets had already been established before that time. They performed those miracles only because the situation demanded it. Since they were so close to Hashem, He fulfilled their wishes, as He promised to the righteous, *"You will decree and it will be fulfilled" (Iyov 22:28)*.

The procedure by which a prophecy can be authenticated I will discuss shortly.

People Claiming to Possess the Power of Prophecy

Those who claim to have the power of prophecy can be divided into two groups,

(a) Those who prophesy in the name of a foreign deity.

(b) Those who prophesy in the name of Hashem.

Those who prophesy in the name of a foreign deity can be classified further into two categories:

(1) The case of a prophet who arises and declares, "A certain star cast a spell over me and told me to worship it in a certain way, or call upon it in a certain way, so that it would save me."

Or the case where a prophet summons **others** to worship Baal or any image, declaring, "An image made itself known to me and told me to command **you** to worship it in a certain manner," as the prophets of Baal and Ashera used to do.

(2) A prophet who says, "The word of Hashem came to me, telling me to worship a given idol, or to influence a certain heavenly constellation for a given purpose." He then tells the people to perform one of the rituals that the Torah classifies as idol worship. This man is also considered as prophesying in the name of a foreign deity, even though he professes to speak in the name of Hashem. For the term "speaking in the name of a foreign deity" includes both a person who claims that the deity itself commanded him to worship it, or one who says that it was G-d who told him to worship any idol.

When a person claiming to be a prophet makes either of these statements, and there are witnesses who will testify to this, then according to Torah law, he must be put to death by strangling, as it says, *"That prophet or dreamer must be put to death."(Devarim* 13:6) We should not even attempt to verify his claim to prophecy, and we should not ask him to perform a sign. Even if he **did** perform amazing signs and wonders as proof of his prophetic powers, he still must be strangled. We should pay no attention to his signs, because the reason these miracles came about is, *"that Hashem is testing you . . ."(Devarim* 13:4). Besides, our intellect which gives the lie to his testimony is more reliable than our eye that sees his miracles. Great thinkers have offered undeniable proof that nothing should be revered and worshipped except the One, the Cause of all existence. He is One, with a Unity that is absolutely unique.

Those who prophesy in the name of Hashem can

also be subdivided into two categories: The false prophet and the true prophet.

The False Prophet

This prophet prophesies in the name of the Almighty, he summons the people to believe in Him, and commands them to worship Him. However he also says that the Holy One, Blessed is He, added a mitzvah or did away with one of the mitzvos of the Torah. He is considered a false prophet and should be put to death by strangling. It makes no difference whether he adds to or detracts from the written Torah verse or adds to or detracts from the traditional oral interpretation.

An example of detracting from a verse would be if he said, "Hashem told me that *orlah* [the prohibition of eating the fruit of newly planted trees for the first three years] applies for only **two years**, and afterwards you are allowed to eat the fruit." An example of adding to a Torah verse would be if he said, "Hashem told me that you are forbidden to eat *orlah* for **four years**," as opposed to what Hashem actually said, *"For **three years** the fruit shall be a forbidden growth, and it may not be eaten" (Vayikra* 19:23). Any similar statement brands him a false prophet.

If he makes the slightest change even in the Oral Law, he is considered a false prophet, even if the plain meaning of the verse seems to support his statement.

For example, it says in the Torah, *"If two men get into a fight with each other, and the wife of one comes up to defend her husband, grabbing his attacker by his private parts, you shall cut off her hand . . ." (Devarim* 25:11,12).

The Oral tradition explains that the statement *"cut off her hand"* should not be taken literally but rather to mean that she should pay a fine for the humiliation she caused her victim. Now if a prophet would say "Hashem told me that the phrase, *'you shall cut off her hand'* is to be understood in its literal sense.", he is a false prophet and must be put to death by strangling, because he attributed to Hashem a statement He never made.

In this case too, we should not pay attention to any sign or miracle this person might perform. The prophet Moshe who awed the whole world with his miracles and convinced us of his legitimacy so that we believed in him, as it is written, *"they will believe in you forever"* (Shemos 19:9), already told us in the name of Hashem that no Law would ever come from the Creator other than that given to Moshe. This idea is derived from the verse *"It [The Torah] is not in heaven...It is in your mouth and in your heart, so that you can keep it"* (Devarim 30:12,14). The phrase *"in your mouth"* refers to the clearly stated Oral Law transmitted by Moshe, whereas the phrase *"in your heart"* refers to the implied laws which were derived through analytical research which is a function of the heart.

We are expressly warned not to add to or detract from the laws of the Torah as it says, *"Be careful to observe everything that I am prescribing to you. Do not add to it and do not subtract from it"* (Devarim 13:1). The Sages therefore said, "A prophet is not allowed to introduce anything new, from now [the time of Moshe] on" (Megillah 2b).

Since we have established that such a claim of prophecy is, in fact, a false statement about Hashem, and that he attributes to Hashem sayings He never uttered, he is liable to the death penalty, as it is writen, *"But any prophet who presumes to speak in My name when I have not commanded him to do so . . .then that prophet shall die"* (*Devarim* 19:20).

The True Prophet

The second kind of prophet who speaks in the name of Hashem is one who calls on the people to worship Hashem, commands them to observe his mitzvos and urges them to keep the Torah without additions or subtractions, as Malachi, the last of the prophets did when he said, "Be mindful of the Torah of My servant Moshe" (*Malachi* 3:22). He promises a rich reward to those who fulfill the commandments of the Torah and warns those who violate it of the dire consequences, as did *Yeshayah, Yirmiyah, Yechezkel* and all the other prophets. In addition, he may tell people to do certain things and forbid them to do other things, regarding matters that are not specifically mentioned in the Torah. For example, he might order the people to attack a certain city or nation, as Shmuel did when he commanded Shaul to attack Amalek (*Shmuel I*, 15); or he might prevent them from killing others, as Elisha did when he prohibited Yehoram from striking down the army of Aram which had entered Shomron (*Melachim II* 6:22). The prophet might do as Yeshayah did when he halted the bringing of water to make cement to repair the cracks in the wall *(Yeshayah* 22:9), or he might act like Yirmiyah who prevented the Jews from going to *Eretz Yisrael* [before the end of the seventy years of exile], (*Yirmiyah* 29:4-10). Many other examples can be cited.

When a prophet claims to have the power of

prophecy without basing it on any foreign source, and without adding to or detracting away from the Torah, but speaks of other matters, like those we have mentioned, then we need to check him out, to verify his testimony. If his testimony proves to be true, then any command he gives should be obeyed, from the smallest to the weightiest matter. Whoever violates one of such a prophet's commands is liable to the death penalty at the hands of the Heavenly Court, as Hashem said about a person who violates the command of a prophet, *"I will punish that person"* (*Devarim* 18:19).

But if this person's claim of being a prophet proves to be untrue, he must be put to death by strangling.

Establishing the Truth of a Prophet's Claim

The truth of a person's claim to being a prophet is established in the following manner:

a) He makes a valid claim to prophecy as was discussed above.

b) He has the characteristics befitting a prophet; he is a scholar, a pious, self-disciplined, intelligent person, and a man of noble character, in keeping with the saying that "Prophecy rests only on one who is wise, strong and rich" (*Shabbos* 92a). (The many qualities of this kind cannot all be listed here. Discussing them and deriving them from their Biblical sources would require a book in itself. Perhaps Hashem will help me to compose what should be written on this subject.)

c) We say to him, "Predict the future for us, and tell

us some of the things Hashem has taught you." He must do so. If his predictions all come true, then we know that his entire prophecy was genuine. But if his prediction does not come true in its entirety, even if it is missing only a minor detail, then we know that he is a false prophet.

This test is described in the Torah, *"You may ask yourselves, 'How can we know that a declaration was not spoken by Hashem?' If the prophet predicts something in Hashem's name, and the prediction does not materialize or come true, then the message was not spoken by Hashem. That prophet has spoken deceitfully, and you must not fear him"* (Devarim 18:21,22).

However, even if one or two of his predictions do come true, we do not yet have proof that his prophecy was genuine. Rather, the matter is left undecided until everything he has declared in the name of Hashem is repeatedly confirmed, over and over again. This is borne out by the story of Shmuel, where we are told that only after it became known that all of Shmuel's predictions had come true, *"All Yisrael, from Dan to Beersheva, knew that Shmuel was trustworthy as a prophet of Hashem"* (Shmuel I 3:20).

The people would not hesitate to ask a prophet for help even regarding personal problems. If it had not been for this practice, Shaul, at the beginning of his career, would have never gone to Shmuel to ask him for help in finding the donkeys he lost (*Shmuel I* 9:3-10). Without a doubt, this was the accepted custom, for Hashem gave us prophets instead of astrologers, fortunetellers and diviners, so that we would ask them for advice of a general nature and about specific problems. They would give us dependable answers, unlike the fortunetellers whose predictions may or may not come true, as it says, *"The nations that you are driving out listen to astrologers and diviners, but what Hashem has given you is totally different. Hashem your G-d will raise up for you a prophet from among your own people, like myself; him you heed"* (*Devarim* 18:15,16).

Because of this power [that the prophet could foresee events] a prophet was called a *ro'eh*, a seer, as it is written, *"for the prophet of today was formerly called a ro'eh, [seer]"* (*Shmuel I* 9:9).

Difference Between Prophecy and the Occult

One should not think, "Since a prophet proves he is genuine by the fact that his predictions come true, then all fortunetellers, astrologers and mind readers can claim to be prophets, because we see with our own eyes that they predict the future every day!"

I want to emphasize that this is an important issue that needs to be clarified so that people clearly understand the sharp difference that exists between the message of a prophet who speaks in the name of Hashem and the words of a fortuneteller.

I want to put it this way: Fortunetellers, astrologers and all others in this category do indeed predict future events, but their predictions are only partially true, while the remainder inevitably turns out to be false. We see this happen all the time, and even the fortunetellers themselves do not deny this. The only way that one fortuneteller is better than the next is that he told fewer lies than his colleague did. But that all of a fortuneteller's predictions should come true, is simply impossible.

These crystal gazers do not even pretend or boast that their predictions will come true in all details. One fortuneteller might say, "This year there will be a drought; there will be no rainfall at all this year," when, in fact, a small amount of rain will fall. Or another might say, "Tomorrow it will rain," while it actually will rain on the day after. And even such a near-miss will happen only to an eminent expert in the art of the occult, one of the authorities who are quoted in books. Yeshayah spoke about these diviners when he challenged Babylonia, *"You are helpless despite all your art. Let them stand up and help you now, the astrologers, the star-gazers, who predict parts of the months' events, whatever will come upon you"* (*Yeshayah* 47:13). Our Rabbis commented that Yeshayah stated, "who predict *parts* of the events," and that he did not state, "who predict those events in their entirety."

The testimonies and predictions of the prophets, however, are altogether different. All their prophesies come true word for word and letter for letter, and not even the slightest detail of anything they say in the name of Hashem remains unfulfilled. Therefore, if any portion of a prophecy does not come true, we know that the man who proclaimed it is an impostor, *"for nothing that Hashem has spoken will remain unfulfilled"* (*Melachim II*, 10:10).

This is what Yirmiyah had in mind when he said that the visions of people who claim to have prophetic power must be proven to be correct in every detail. He would discredit the false prophets and demolish their claims to prophecy, saying, *"Let the prophet who has a dream tell the dream; and let him who has received My word report My word faithfully! How can straw be compared to grain?" says Hashem* (*Yirmiyah* 23:28).The Sages explain this to mean that prophecy is crystal clear without any elements of falsehood blended in, just as grain kernels are separate from straw. The dreams of the fortune-tellers are mostly false, like straw that contains a few kernels of wheat. "Just as it is impossible to have grain without straw, so too it is impossible [for an ordinary person] to have a dream without senseless matters" (*Berachos* 55a).

Threatening Predictions

There still remains one important point on which we should comment, namely, if a prophet foretells catastrophic events such as famine, war, earthquakes, a disastrous hail storm or similar calamities, as a punishment to the people. Heaven may have mercy, and the punishment will not arrive. In fact everything will remain peaceful and quiet. This does not mean that the prophet lied. It would be incorrect to say that he is a false prophet and deserving the death penalty, because although a punishment was decreed, Hashem abrogated the decree. It may very well be that the people repented of their despicable behavior, or that Hashem mercifully postponed their punishment and will show His anger at another time, as He did with Achav when He said through Eliyahu, *"I will not bring the disaster in his lifetime; I will bring the disaster upon his house in his son's time"* (*Melachim I* 21:29). Or He may have had pity on them because of good deeds they did earlier. The statement, *"The prediction does not materialize or come true"* (*Devarim* 18:21) [which is the sign of a false prophet] does not apply to this prophet.

Good Tidings

However, if the prophet forecasts tidings of good things to occur at a set time, and he says, "This will be a year of quiet and tranquility," yet a war breaks out; or if he predicts, "This will be a year of rain and blessing," but famine and drought occur, then we know that he is a false prophet, and his fraudulent claim to prophecy is exposed. This is expressed in the verse, *"The prophet has spoken deceitfully, and you must not fear him"* (*Devarim* 18:21), meaning, "do not let him frighten you or terrify you into refraining from killing him, [by reminding you of] his piety, righteousness and wisdom. He is guilty of brazenly making such a momentous declaration and speaking rebelliously against Hashem. For when Hashem sends good tidings through a prophet, it is impossible to say that He will not fulfill His promise, for He will certainly confirm the promise the prophet made to the people. Our Sages put it this way, "Any good tidings Hashem announces, even if it is subject to certain conditions, He does not go back on" (*Berachos* 7a).

Now there is the puzzling fact that *Yaakov* [as he returned to Eretz Yisrael and Esav was preparing to attack him] feared for his life, as it says, *"Yaakov was very frightened and distressed"* (*Bereishis* 32:8), even though Hashem had assured him of good fortune, saying, *"I am with you. I will protect you wherever you go"* (*Bereishis* 28:15). The Sages explain that Yaakov was afraid that he had committed a sin which would cause his death (*Berachos* 4a).

This incident teaches us that although Hashem promises good fortune to someone, his sins may stand in the way and these promises may not be realized. But we must realize that this will only happen in matters that are between Hashem and the prophet alone, but when Hashem tells a prophet to bring good tidings to other people in a definite and unconditional message, then for this good not to come about is absurd and unthinkable. Otherwise, we have no way of establishing the genuineness of anyone's prophetic message; yet Hashem gave us in His Torah the fundamental principle that the proof of a prophet's genuineness is in the fact that his predictions come true.

It was this fundamental principle that Yirmiyah referred to in his dispute with Chananiah ben Azur. Yirmiyah was prophesying disaster and death, declaring that Nebuchadnezzar would be victorious and succeed in destroying the *Beis Hamikdash*. Chananiah ben Azur was predicting good tidings, that the vessels of the Beis Hamikdash which had been carted off to Babylonia would be returned to Yerushalayim. During the ensuing debate Yirmiyah said that if his own prediction would not come true, and Nebuchadnezzar would not be victorious and the vessels would be returned to the Beis Hamikdash, as Chananiah said would happen, this would not disprove his own (Yirmiyah's) prophecy, for it is possible that Hashem had mercy on the people. But if Chananiah's predictions would not come true, and the vessels would **not** be returned to the Beis Hamikdash, this will be clear proof that Chananiahs prophecy was false. Chananiah's prophetic mission would only be established when all his predictions of good fortune came true.

"But listen to this word which I address to you and to all the people. The prophets who lived before you and me from ancient times prophesied war, disaster and pestilence against many lands and great kingdoms. If a prophet prophesies good fortune, when the word of the prophet comes true it will be known that Hashem really sent him" (*Yirmiyah 28:7-9*). What Yirmiyah means to say is that we cannot tell by

the bad tidings of prophets whether they are true or false prophets. But we **do** know with certainty that they are true prophets if they foretell good fortune and their promises come true.

The Prophet's Powers and Restrictions

When a prophet's predictions have come true according to the guidelines we have established, and that prophet becomes famous like Shmuel, Eliyahu and others, that prophet has the power to modify the Torah in a way that no one else may do. If he would order the cancellation of any of the positive commandments of the Torah, or he would permit something that is forbidden by a negative commandment, as a temporary emergency measure, then as long as it is not a command to worship idols, it is our duty to obey him and to carry out his command. Whoever violates his orders will be put to death by Hashem. The Sages of the Talmud stated this clearly:

"Regarding any matter, if a prophet tells you to violate the words of the Torah, you should obey him; except for idol worship" (*Sanhedrin* 90a).

However, this is only true provided that it is not a permanent ruling. He may not say that Hashem has decreed that this mitzvah be nullified forever. He may only order a suspension of a mitzvah for a temporary need. That prophet himself, when asked about his order to violate one of the mitzvos that Hashem gave us through Moshe, will answer that the suspension of this mitzvah is not permanent but only a temporary measure for the present moment. This is similar to the power that the *Beis Din* [Rabbinical High Court] has to issue an emergency order, to temporarily nullify certain Mitzvos. Eliyahu made use of this principle when he sacrificed on Mount Carmel (*Melachim* I, 18:20-40), while the Beis Hamikdash was standing. Doing such a thing without the command of a prophet is punishable by *kares* [premature death]. The Torah cautions against this, stating, *"Be careful not to offer your burnt offerings in any place that you may see fit"* (*Devarim* 12:13). And we are told that a person who offers a sacrifice outside of Yerushalayim is subject to kares in the verse, *"Bloodguilt shall be counted for that man; he has spilled blood; that man shall be cut off from among his people"* (*Vayikra* 17:4).

If anyone had asked Eliyahu at the time he was offering the sacrifice on Mount Carmel, "Are we allowed to do such a thing from now on?" he would have answered that it was not permitted, and anyone offering sacrifices outside the Beis Hamikdash was liable to kares, but that the present ceremony was a one-time emergency action designed to expose the falsehood of the prophets of Baal and to smash their pagan belief.

In the same way, the prophet Elisha, when ordering an attack on Moab, decreed the cutting of every fruit-bearing tree, *"You shall cut down every good tree"* (*Melachim* II 3:19), although Hashem prohibited this in the Torah, stating, *"You must not destroy its trees, wielding an ax against any food producing tree"* (*Devarim* 20:19). Now, if people had asked Elisha whether this prohibition had been lifted, and it was permitted from now on to cut down fruit bearing trees when laying siege to a city, he would have replied that it was not permitted, and that the present decree was a one-time emergency measure.

Let me give you an illustration which will explain to you the this principle as it applies to all the mitzvos.

Suppose a prophet whose credentials are impeccable

told us on Shabbos that all B'nei Yisrael—men and women alike—should light a fire, make weapons with it, put on battle attire and attack a certain place on this Shabbos day, and that we should plunder the enemies' possessions and take their women captive. As Torah-observers we would have the duty to get up immediately, and do as he told us, with eagerness and extraordinary love, without qualms or reservations. And we must believe that with whatever we were doing, whether it was making a fire, performing forbidden labors, killing the enemy or fighting a war, we were performing a mitzvah, notwithstanding that it was Shabbos. We should expect to be richly rewarded for it by Hashem because by fulfilling a command of a prophet we are observing a positive commandment, *"Hashem your G-d will raise up for you a prophet from among your own people,* **and it is to him that you must listen"** (*Devarim* 18:15). The Oral Law expounded on this verse, "In all matters, if a prophet tells you to violate the words of the Torah, you should listen to him—except for idol worship" (*Sanhedrin* 90a). For example, if he told you, "Worship this image only today," or, "Burn incense for this star only for this hour," he must be killed, and no one should listen to him.

Conversely, take the case of a person who considers himself a righteous and G-d-fearing man. He is old, well advanced in years, and he says to himself, "I have reached old age, and never in my life have I transgressed any of the mitzvos. How can I go and commit on this Shabbos a transgression for which the penalty is stoning? How can I go out to fight in the war? After all, I cannot contribute anything to the outcome. Let them find others to take my place; there are many others who can do it!"

This man is a rebel, he is breaking Hashem's law, and for violating the prophet's command he incurs death by G-d's hand. He Who commanded us to keep the Shabbos commanded us to obey the words and decrees of the prophet, as it is written, *"If any person shall not listen to the word that he declares in My name, I will punish that person"* (*Devarim* 18:19).

All the same, if, while doing the work on Shabbos that the prophet has commanded, a person tied a double knot [which is one of the 39 labors that are forbidden on Shabbos], that was not needed for that work, then he is liable for stoning.

If this same prophet who commanded us as he did and we obeyed him, would tell us that the Shabbos boundary is one *amah* less or one *amah* more than two thousand *amas*, [thereby changing one of the laws of Shabbos] claiming that he received this knowledge by way of prophecy rather than through Scriptural analysis and logical argument, then we know that he is a false prophet and must be executed by strangling.

This illustration gives you the means of understanding what a prophet may command you and of grasping all that is written in the Torah on the subject of a prophet who contradicts any part of the mitzvos. This fundamental principle is the key to understanding the entire subject matter, and it is only in this respect [temporary emergency measure] that a prophet is different from other people, regarding mitzvos. But as far as deriving mitzvos through analysis, logical reasoning and deductive thinking is concerned he is on the same level as the other sages who do not possess prophetic powers. If a prophet advances a logical argument in support of a halachic ruling and someone who is not a prophet likewise advances a different rational argument, but the prophet declares, "Hashem told me that my reasoning is correct," you should not pay attention to him. And even if one thousand prophets of the caliber of Eliyahu and Elisha would support one line of reasoning and one thousand and one sages would support an opposing logic, we would follow the majority, and the Halachah would be decided according to the view of the one thousand and one sages, and **not** according to the one thousand honorable prophets.

The Sages of the Talmud said it like this, "By G-d! Even if Yehoshua bin Nun personally would tell this to me I would not listen to him or pay attention to him" (*Chullin* 124a).

They also said, "If Eliyahu would come and say, '*Chalitzah* should be performed with a shoe,' listen to him, but if he would say, 'with a sandal', then do not listen to him" (*Yevamos* 102a).

What they mean to say is that under no circumstances may anything be added to or taken away from the mitzvos on the basis of prophecy. Similarly, if a prophet declared that Hashem told him that the practical application of a given mitzvah is such-and-such, and that the rationale offered by one sage rather than that of another is correct, then this prophet must be put to death because he is a false prophet, as we have established as a fundamental rule: No Torah was given after the first prophet Moshe, and nothing may be added or taken away from it, as it says, "*It is not in heaven*" [*requiring prophetic insight*] (*Devarim* 30:12). Hashem did not permit us to learn the Torah laws from the prophets, but only from the Sages, men who derive the law from logical inferences and opinions. Hashem does not say, "*If you are unable to reach a decision . . . you must approach the prophet who exists at the time*" but rather, "*You must approach the Kohanim-Levi'im [and other members of] the supreme court that exists at the time*" (*Devarim* 17:9). The Sages have discussed this subject extensively, and this is a true presentation of their views.

The Transmission of the Oral Torah

When *Yehoshua* bin Nun was nearing his death, he taught the elders the oral explanation that he had received from Moshe. He also transmitted to them the new applications of the laws that were agreed upon by all the Sages and those laws that were not agreed upon by all the Sages but were decided by a majority vote of the elders.

This, that the elders received the oral tradition from Yehoshua is referred to in the verse, *"Yisrael served Hashem during the lifetime of Yehoshua and the lifetime of the elders who lived on after Yehoshua, and who had experienced all that Hashem had done for Yisrael"* (*Yehoshua* 24:31). In the following generation these elders taught the prophets all that they had received from Yehoshua. Each prophet in turn taught the next. During all this time there was constant analysis of the law and new laws were derived according to the established rules.

The sages of each generation regarded the teachings of the earlier sages as authoritative. They would study them and extract new ideas from them, but they would never disagree with them. This process of transmission continued until the era of the Men of the

Great Assembly [a legislative body consisting of 120 Sages], including in its ranks [the prophets] Chaggai, Zechariah, Malachi, Daniel, Chananiah, Mishael, Azariah, Ezra HaSofer, Nechemiah ben Chachalyah, Mordechai and Zerubavel ben She'altiel. The remainder of the 120 Sages were comprised of the [elite Torah scholars referred to in the Scriptures (Melachim II 24:16) as the] "craftsmen and locksmiths" [in reference to their profound scholarship]. Like their predecessors, they too, researched the Oral Tradition, enacted precautionary decrees to prevent violations of the law, and issued ordinances.

The last of this illustrious group was one of the earliest sages mentioned in the Mishnah; Shimon Hatzaddik who was the *Kohein Gadol* of that generation.

Rabbi Yehudah Hanassi [Rebbi]

In the course of time, *Rabbeinu Hakadosh* arrived on the scene, a personality who was outstanding in his generation and unique in his time; a man of such perfect piety and sterling character, that his contemporaries called him *Rabbeinu Hakadosh*—Our Holy Teacher. His name was Rabbi Yehudah [Hanassi—the Prince. He was affectionately called Rebbi-our teacher—because he was regarded by all as their teacher]. He was supreme in wisdom and grandeur, to the extent that the Talmud says of him, "From Moshe until Rebbi, we do not find Torah scholarship and majesty combined in one person" (*Gittin* 59a). He exemplified piety and humility, and shunned all pleasures of life, as it says, "Since Rebbi died, humility and fear of sin have vanished" (*Sotah* 49a). He expressed himself clearly and surpassed everyone in his command of the holy tongue, to the point that the Sages learned the meaning of Biblical words about which they were in doubt from the way his servants and maids used these words. This is mentioned in a well-known passage in the Talmud (*Rosh Hashanah* 26b). He was immensely wealthy and wielded great power, so that people said about him, "Rebbi's butler is wealthier than Shabor, the king of Persia" (*Bava Metzia* 85a). He relieved the plight of needy scholars and students and spread Torah knowledge among the Jewish people. He collected the oral tradition, including the words of the Sages and their conflicting views that were handed down since the days of Moshe Rabbeinu until his own time.

He himself was a link in the chain of transmission of the Oral Torah, since he received it from his father, *Rabbi Shimon III*, and *Shimon III* received it from his father *Rabban Gamliel II*, who received it from *Rabban Shimon II*, who received it from *Hillel*; he from *Shemayah* and *Avtalyon*; they from *Yehudah ben Tabbai* and *Shimon ben Shetach*; they from *Yehoshua ben Perachyah* and *Nitai* of *Arbela*; they from *Yosei ben Yo'ezer* and *Yosei ben Yochanan*; they from *Antignos Ish Socho*; he from *Shimon Hatzaddik*, who received it from *Ezra* and the Men of the Great Assembly. *Ezra* received the Oral Torah from *Baruch ben Neriah* his teacher, *Baruch* from *Yirmiyah*, and in the same way, *Yirmiyah* definitely received it from the prophets that went before him, reaching back from prophet to prophet to the elders who received the Oral Torah from *Yehoshua bin Nun* who, in turn, received it from *Moshe*.

Categories of the Oral Torah

After collecting all the opinions and the statements of the previous Sages, Rabbi Yehudah Hanassi began to compile the Mishnah. He incorporated into the Mishnah the explanation of all the mitzvos of the Torah. Some of these are explanations that were received directly from Moshe, as well as expositions and laws that had not been learned from tradition but had been added by the use of the Thirteen Principles by which the Torah is expounded. Of these, there were some that were agreed upon by all, and others about which differences of opinion had arisen between two authorities. Rabbi Yehudah Hanassi would record these disputes, writing, "This Rabbi says this, but That Rabbi says that." Even if the majority opinion was opposed by only one rabbi, Rabbi Yehudah Hanassi would record the single dissenting opinion and the majority view. He did this for very important reasons which are mentioned in the Mishnah in *Eiduyos* (1:6). I will refer to them later [page 40] but first I must discuss a very basic principle:

Halachah leMoshe miSinai

[The Talmud refers to certain laws as *Halachah leMoshe miSinai*—accepted tradition received directly from Moshe at Sinai and as such, not open to debate]. You may wonder, if all the explanations of the laws of the Torah were received from Moshe, as we are taught,"the general principles, the specifics and the details of each law of the Torah were told on Mount Sinai"(*Toras Kohanim, Vayikra* 25:1) [as outlined above (page 2)], then in what way are the laws that are known as *Halachah leMoshe miSinai* different than all other laws?

Let me explain this elementary issue very clearly:

[In regard to the fact that tradition handed down from Moshe is accepted as reliable and not open for debate, there is no distinction between *Halachah leMoshe miSinai* and other explanations handed down from Moshe.] Therefore, there never existed an argument about the basic interpretation of the verses of the Torah. There never has arisen a dispute among authorities of any time or era—from Moshe until Rav Ashi [who finalized the Talmud]—in which one sage would say that the phrase *"an eye for an eye" (Devarim* 19:21) should be taken literally, and another sage would say that the Torah is referring to monetary compensation.

Likewise, there never arose a dispute over the meaning of the verse, *"On the first day you shall take the fruit of a hadar tree,"* (*Vayikra* 23:40), whereby one sage said that this fruit was an *esrog*, and another said that it referred to a quince, a pomegranate or some other fruit.

Nor have we come across an argument about the fact that *anaf eitz avos*, "branches of an *avos* tree"

(*Vayikra* 23:40) refers to myrtle branches, or a disagreement about the fact that *"you must cut off her hand"* (*Devarim* 25:12) is not to be taken literally but means monetary compensation.

Similarly, no one ever disputed the fact that the death sentence in the verse, *"If a kohein's daughter defiles herself by acting promiscuously . . . she must be burned with fire"* (*Vayikra* 21:9) is carried out only if she was a married woman. In line with this, no one—from Moshe until today—has ever denied that the punishment of stoning for a girl who was found not to have been a virgin, (*Devarim* 22:20) applied only if she was a married woman, and witnesses testified that after her betrothal she committed adultery in their presence and that they had warned her beforehand. There is no disagreement about these and similar commandments, because the explanations of all these laws were received from Moshe. It is with regard to such mitzvos that the Sages said, "The general outline and the specifics of the entire Torah were told on Sinai."

However, although these explanations were received from Moshe and cannot be disputed, we can trace these explanations to the Torah text by means of the rules of Torah interpretation, through reasoning, comparisons, proofs and allusions.

When you find the Sages in the Talmud disagreeing with one another, bringing proofs for any of these explanations or others like it, they are not arguing over the validity of the explanation, but rather how this explanation is derived from the text itself. For example, when they discuss the meaning of the term "fruit of a *hadar* tree," Some Rabbis bring Scriptural proof from the juxtaposition in the text of the words "fruit" and "tree" to indicate that it must be the fruit of a tree whose bark tastes the same as its fruit [which is true of the esrog]. Another Sage finds a hint for the esrog in the word *hadar*, explaining that the word *hadar* can be interpreted to mean—*that dwells*; it is a fruit that dwells in the tree from year to year, which can only be an esrog. A third Sage, noting a kinship between *hadar* and the Greek *hydor*, meaning water, says that it is a fruit that grows on much water—an esrog. The Rabbis did not bring these proofs because they were not sure of what the Torah meant by "fruit of *hadar*" until these hints were found. Of course, ever since the days of Yehoshua, Jews took a *lulav* and an *esrog* in hand, year after year; there was no quarrel about that. The Rabbis merely searched for a hint in the Torah for this accepted tradition. The same is true for the proofs the Rabbis brought for the *hadas* [myrtle branch], and their proofs for the law requiring monetary restitution for inflicting bodily injury (*Bava Kamma* 83), as well as their proof for the law concerning the death penalty for a *kohein's* daughter who had committed adultery (*Sanhedrin* 50b).

All proofs like these are meant to serve as Scriptural allusions to well-known and long-established traditions. This is the meaning of the statement, "The general outlines and the specifics were told on Sinai." In other words, those matters that can be drawn out from the text through the rule of *k'lal up'rat*, "a general statement limited by a specification" or through any of the other Rules of Interpretation, were handed down to us by Moshe who received them on Sinai.

Although we received all these laws from Moshe, we do not call them *Halachah leMoshe miSinai*—Laws Given to Moshe on Sinai. You cannot say that the tradition that *peri eitz hadar* means an *esrog*, or the law that if someone wounds his fellow Jew, he must pay monetary compensation are *Halachah leMoshe miSinai*, because although all these explanations came to us from Moshe, there are indications for them in the text or they have been derived by logical analysis, as we have mentioned. Only those laws for which no hint or allusion can be found in Scripture and cannot be derived from the text by means of one of the methods of interpretation, are termed *Halachah leMoshe miSinai*.

This is the reason why when it was said that "Legal measurements are *Halachah leMoshe miSinai*", the question was raised, "How can you say that legal measurements are *Halachah leMoshe miSinai* when legal measurements are alluded to in the verse, *"It is a land of wheat, barley, grapes, figs and pomegranates, a land of oil olives and honey dates?"* (*Devarim* 8:8). The answer was: Legal measurements are indeed *Halachah leMoshe miSinai*, and they cannot logically be derived from the verse; there is not even a suggestion for them anywhere in the Torah. The association of legal measurements with this verse is only a way to jog the memory and make it easier to remember them; it has nothing to do with the actual meaning of the verse. This is what the Sages meant whenever they said, "It is merely an *asmachta*", a mnemonic device.

Now I will list most—and possibly all—of the laws that are termed *Halachah leMoshe miSinai*. You will then realize that what I said was correct, that not one of these laws has been derived from the Torah by means of logical reasoning, and that none of them can be related to a Scriptural verse, except as a way of jogging the memory. We do not find that the Rabbis analyzed these laws or brought proofs for them. The Rabbis learned them from Moshe, exactly as Hashem had instructed him.

The List of Halachos leMoshe miSinai

1. The measurement of one-half log of oil needed to be mixed with the loaves that are presented along with a thanksgiving offering (*Vayikra* 7:12).

2. The measurement of one-fourth log of oil needed for the loaves offered by a *nazir* when the term of his nazirite vow is complete.

3. The law that there are eleven days between two *niddah* periods.

4. The law that a wall is considered as being extended vertically under certain condition.

5. The law that an empty space of less than three handbreadth wide separating a solid surface is considered as solid surface.

6. The law that a ceiling may be considered as a part of the wall from which it extends.

7. Minimum quantities, sizes and measurements.

8. Definition of what constitutes a separation between one's body and the water of a *mikveh*.

9. Minimum dimensions of a partition.

10. The parchment required for the *tefillin*.

11. The parchment required for a *mezuzah* scroll.

12. The parchment required for a Torah scroll.

13. The form of the letter *shin* on the head *tefillin*.

14. The formation of the knot on the straps of the head and arm *tefillin*.

15. The requirement of black straps for *tefillin*.

16. The requirement for *tefillin* to be shaped like a cube.

17. The requirement of a sleeve on the bases of the *tefillin* boxes through which the leather straps are pulled.

18. The requirement that the parchments are tied in

a roll with threads made from the hair of kosher animals, before being placed in the *tefillin* boxes.

19. The requirement that the compartments of the *tefillin* be sewn together with threads made from parts of kosher animals.

20. The composition of the ink that must be used in writing a Torah scroll.

21. The requirement that there be ruled guidelines etched above the lettering in a Torah Scroll.

22. The rule that a girl under the age of three years and one day retains her status of virginity despite cohabitation.

23. The rule that the number of *pei'ah* gifts from a field on which more than one kind of grain is growing depends on whether the different grains are stored together or separately. [*Pei'ah* 2:5]

24. The law that even a seed so fine that a small amount will suffice to plant an entire field, has the same rule as other seeds-insofar as the rule that they are considered insignificant in a mixture when there is less than one twenty-fourth. [*Kilayim* 2:2]

25. Although in a standard field the restriction of plowing begins prior to the actual *sh'mittah* [sabbatical] year, if the field contains at least ten saplings the entire field may be plowed up to the beginning of the *sh'mittah year*. [*Shevi'is* 1:6]

26. If a ring of figs is partly *tamei* [ritually unclean], one may give the full percentage of *terumah* due from both the *tamei* and *tahor* parts, from the *tahor* part alone.[*Terumos* 2:1]

27. On Shabbos, the teacher may find the place by lamplight from which the students are to begin reading.[*Shabbos* 1:3]

28. A woman must bring a sin offering if she carries an object in her apron on Shabbos, even if she placed the object in the front of her apron, and it inadvertently moved to her back. [*Shabbos* 10:4]

29. The right of a wine seller to mix strong wine into his soft wine without being guilty of deception (since he is improving the product).[Bava Metzia 4:11]

30. The law that Jews living in Ammon and Moab must give *ma'aseir ani* [the tithe for the needy] in the seventh year.

Whenever we will come across one of these laws in our Commentary on the Mishnah we will elaborate on it, with G-d's help.

Five Categories of the Oral Law

The Oral Law can now be divided into five categories:

1. Explanations that were received directly from Moshe, that are hinted at in the verse, and that can be drawn from text by means of logical reasoning. Such laws may not be disputed, and when someone says, "This is what I received," there can be no further debate.

2. The laws which are known as *Halachah leMoshe miSinai*, and which cannot be proven as we explained. These laws may not be disputed either.

3. Laws that were derived by reasoning, about which there may arise differences of opinion, as we mentioned earlier. In such cases, the law is decided on the basis of the majority vote. Such disputes come about when different rational approaches are used. Therefore the Rabbis say, "If it is a stated Halachah

CATEGORIES OF THE ORAL TORAH

then we must accept it, but if it is open for discussion let us debate it" (*Yevamos* 8:3).

Disputes arose only regarding matters about which no clear cut *Halachah* was received. Throughout the entire Talmud you find the Sages looking for the underlying reasons for the disputes among the earlier authorities. They will ask, "What is the point at issue?" or, "What reason does This Rabbi give?" or, "What is the practical difference between them?" In most instances the Sages answer these questions, giving the reason for the dispute. They might say, for example, "This Rabbi holds this for such a reason, and That Rabbi holds that because of another reason."

Do not think for a moment that the Sages received the disputed laws from Moshe, or that the conflicts arose because some Sages made errors or were forgetful, or that one Sage heard the law correctly and his opponent heard it incorrectly, or forgot it, or heard it only partially. And do not try to defend your [mistaken] theory by quoting the saying, "Ever since a growing number of students of Hillel and Shammai did not study under their teachers sufficiently, disputes increased in Yisrael, and the Torah came to be understood two different ways" (*Sanhedrin* 88b). To say such a thing is disgraceful. Only an ignorant and unlearned person would say this, a person who does not understand the fundamentals of Judaism and who slurs the people from whom we received the commandments. Such statements amount to empty talk; they are without rhyme or reason. What brings people to believe such false ideas is that they did not study the words of the Sages in the Talmud sufficiently. Although they correctly concluded that explanations came from Moshe, they failed to draw a distinction between those basic explanations that were explicitly given by Moshe and those details and offshoots the Sages themselves derived through their own analysis.

Now, when it comes to the controversy between *Beis Shammai* and *Beis Hillel* over whether "you should clear the table first and then you rinse your hands," or, "you should rinse your hands first and then clear the table" (*Berachos* 51b), don't let it enter your mind that either one of these statements was relayed to us directly by Moshe. The underlying reason for *Beis Shammai* and *Beis Hillel's* dispute is mentioned in the Talmud: one of them forbids us to employ an ignorant servant and the other does not[1]. [Their argument is obviously not what was handed down from Moshe, rather based on logical arguments.] All similar controversies should be understood the same way.

Let us explain the statement, "Ever since a growing number of students of Hillel and Shammai did not study sufficiently, disputes increased in Yisrael." If you have two men with the same intelligence, thinking power and knowledge of the basic facts from which to draw conclusions, they will have very few, if any, disagreements. Shammai and Hillel, who disagreed on only a few laws are an example of this. They thought along the same lines when it came to deriving new laws, and they both interpreted the basic facts the same way. But when the students became less interested in learning and their reasoning became blurred in comparison to their teachers Hillel and Shammai, then often disputes surfaced between them based

---

1. We are concerned that water might drip from the hands and spoil pieces of bread that are lying on the table. Beis Hillel forbids the use of an ignorant servant who does not know to remove the larger pieces of bread. Therefore, Beis Hillel states that it is not necessary to clear the table before rinsing the hands. Beis Shammai permits the use of an ignorant servant, so they require that the table be cleared before rinsing your hands.

upon their analysis of the many laws. Each one made assumptions according to his own reasoning power and according to his understanding of the basic principles.

Still, we should not find fault in them because of this. For we cannot ask of two sages that they conduct their debate on the intellectual level of Yehoshua and Pinchas. Neither do we harbor any doubt about the things that they disagreed on, even though they are not as great as Shammai and Hillel were, or as sages who were even greater. For Hashem did not command us to serve Him in such a way [demanding that we obey only those sages who are as great as the early sages], but He did command us to obey the sages of our own generation, as it says, *"You must approach the judge that exists at that time"* (*Devarim* 17:9).

This was the way conflicts arose; not because scholars erred regarding the tradition handed down from Moshe, and that one was right and the other wrong. If you think about it, it will become crystal clear to you, and you will realize what a precious and great ground rule about the mitzvos this is.

[In the following category the Rambam discusses those parts of the Oral Law that are not explanations of the Written Law.]

4. Preventive measures that the prophets and sages established in each generation, in order to "make a hedge" for the Torah. Hashem ordered them to issue such preventive measure, which fall under the heading of, *"Safeguard My charges,"* (*Vayikra* 18:30), which the Oral Law explains to mean, "Make precautions to protect My charges" (*Yevamos* 21a). The Sages called these preventive measures *gezeiros*.

Disputes sometimes arose about these *gezeiros*. One

Sage might prohibit something as a precaution and another disagreed with him. You find this very often in the Talmud where it will say: "This Rabbi prohibited such-and-such because of this-and-that, and That Rabbi did not." This is another one of the various causes of disputes. For example, the Torah forbids only the mixing of dairy products with meat of an animal. The Sages prohibited mixing poultry with dairy products in order to prevent an unintentional violation of the Torah prohibition through the confusion of poultry with meat. There was one Sage, Rabbi Yosei Hagelili, who did not impose this decree, and who permitted eating poultry with milk, and the people of his city ate the two together, as related in the Talmud (*Chullin* 116a).

Once a *gezeirah* is adopted by the Sages, no one is allowed to oppose it in any way shape or form. And once a *gezeirah* becomes widely accepted among all the Jewish people it can never be revoked. Not even a prophet was allowed to nullify a *gezeirah*. In this connection we read in the Talmud that "Eliyahu would have been unable to annul any of the eighteen *gezeiros* that were instituted by *Beis Shammai* and *Beis Hillel*," and the reason given was, "that their prohibitions were widely accepted throughout Yisrael" (*Avodah Zarah* 36a).

5. Laws that were enacted by the Rabbis in order to preserve harmony among the people, which neither add to or take away from any mitzvah and practices which would be useful in promoting Torah observance. These enactments are called *takkanos* and *minhagim* [customs], and you are forbidden to disregard either of them. *Shlomoh* had this to say about anyone ignoring them, "*He who breaches a fence will be bitten by a snake*" (*Koheles* 10:8).

The Talmud and the Mishnah mention a great many of these *takkanos*, some of them dealing with ritual matters and others with monetary issues. Some were enacted by prophets like Moshe, Yehoshua, and Ezra, as it says, "Moshe established for the Jews the practice of inquiring and holding lectures on the subject matter of the day: the laws of Pesach on Pesach etc." (*Megillah* 4a), and Moshe composed the first *berachah* of *Birchas Hamazone* in gratitude for the manna with which Hashem sustained Yisrael in the desert (*Berachos* 48b). There are many takkanos that were enacted by Yehoshua and Ezra.

Some *takkanos* are associated with individual Sages, as it says, "Hillel made the *takkanah* of *pruzbul*" (*Shevi'is* 10:3); Rabban Gamliel the Elder decreed. . . ; Rabbi Yochanan ben Zakkai decreed . . . (*Rosh Hashanah* 4:1). There are many examples of this in the Talmud.

Other *takkanos* are linked to the full assembly of the Sages of the Mishnah. Such *takkanos* are introduced with the phrase, "In Usha they enacted. . .," or "The Sages enacted. . .," or "This is an enactment of the Sages . . .," or similar statements.

To sum it up, the laws that are recorded in the Mishnah can be divided into these five categories:

1. Explanations that were received from Moshe, but which are also hinted at in the Torah, or which can be derived from the verse.

2. *Halachah leMoshe miSinai.*

3. Laws that were extracted by comparing and analyzing the text; about these laws there have been disputes.

4. *Gezeiros*, preventive measures.

5. *Takkanos*.

Dissenting Opinions

Rabbi Yehudah Hanassi, the compiler of the Mishnah, found it necessary to include the opinions of both sides to a dispute. Had he only written the final decisions, leaving out the opinions that were rejected, this could raise serious problems. It could happen that one who had received a contradictory Halachah from a Sage who held an opposing view, might cause us to wonder, "How could this man, who obviously is a trustworthy person, receive a tradition that a certain food is forbidden, when the Mishnah says that it is permitted; or vice versa, that something is permitted when the Mishnah says it is forbidden?"

Now that the opposing view is also written in the Mishnah, such misunderstandings will not happen. For if someone should say, "I have heard that such-and-such is forbidden," we will be able to tell him, "You are quite right; what you have heard is indeed the opinion of one Rabbi, but the majority disagreed with him," or, "Another Rabbi disagreed with him, and the Halachah was decided according to the other Rabbi, either because his reasoning was more logical, or because we found another opinion supporting him" (Eiduyos 1:6).

Rabbi Yehudah Hanassi also felt it was necessary to record the opinion of an individual even when the opposing view was the majority view. This was because the final law may eventually be decided according to the individual. The fact that he did so teaches us that if an individual's argument is clear and straightforward, we should listen to it, even if a large number of people oppose it.

He also recorded the original opinion of a Sage who later changed his mind. For example, *"Beis Shammai* say one thing, and *Beis Hillel* say something else, but Beis Hillel changed their mind and agreed with Beis Shammai" (*Eiduyos* 1:2). He did this to show how much they loved the truth, and in order to promote righteousness and integrity. These men were respected, pious, noble and very learned, yet when one realized that his opponent's reasoning was better than his own, and his opponent's analysis was correct, he admitted it. Certainly, we too, should admit when we are wrong and should not be stubborn.

This is what the Torah means when it says, *"Pursue perfect honesty"* (*Devarim* 16:20), and the Sages comment on this, "Acknowledge the truth" (Avos 5:9), meaning, "Although you could defend yourself through convincing arguments; if you know that your opponent's claims are right, but that he is intimidated or that you have greater verbal skill and can convince him that you are correct, withdraw your opinion and accept his."

The Structure of the Mishnah

The Six Orders of the Mishnah

When Rabbi Yehudah HaNasi edited and compiled the Mishnah he divided his work into six parts; he called each part a *Seder* [order].

The first Seder is called **Seder Zera'im** [Seeds], which deals with *mitzvos* that apply to agriculture, like *kilayim* (mingled seeds), *sh'mittah* (the sabbatical year), *orlah* (fruit of a tree in the first three years after planting), *terumos* (contributions of produce given to *kohanim*), and *ma'aseros* (tithe given to the *levi'im*), and other obligatory contributions.

The second is **Seder Mo'eid** [Festivals], which deals with mitzvos relating to the Festivals, the specific obligations of each individual Yom Tov and the things that are forbidden and permitted on each Yom Tov, and all other laws pertaining to the Festivals.

The third is **Seder Nashim** [Women], which is concerned with the laws of marriage, and the different precepts that involve men and women, for example, *yibbum* (levirate marriage), *chalitzah* (the ceremony of removing the obligation of *yibbum*), *kesuvah* (the writing of a marriage contract), *kiddushin* (the betrothal ceremony), *gittin* (writ of divorce), and all other laws that belong in this category.

The fourth is **Seder Nezikin** [Damages], which discusses civil laws, the settling of disputes concerning ownerships, business transactions, partnerships in real estate, and similar issues.

The fifth is **Seder Kodashim** [Sacred Objects], which deals with the sacrifices that are offered in the *Beis Hamikdash*.

The sixth is **Seder Teharos** [Ritual Purity] which discusses the laws of ritual purity of objects used for holy purposes, and what renders them ritually impure.

Rabbi Yehudah Hanasi began the Mishnah with *Seder Zera'im* because it deals with agriculture—the source of sustenance of all life. Man, who was created to serve Hashem, needs food to stay alive. Therefore, Rabbi Yehudah HaNasi opened the Mishnah with the laws dealing with agriculture.

Next in line he placed *Seder Mo'eid*, in keeping with the sequence in which these subjects are arranged in the Torah. First we read about agriculture, *"You may plant your land for six years and gather its crops. But during the seventh year, you must leave it alone and withdraw from it"* (*Shemos* 23:10-11). This is followed by the laws concerning Shabbos and Yom Tov, *"You may do whatever you must during the six weekdays, but you must stop on the seventh day . . .Celebrate for me three festivals in the year"* (*Shemos* 23:12,14).

He then arranged *Seder Nashim* (Women) ahead of *Seder Nezikin* (Damages), in line with the order of the verses: *"If a man sells his daughter as a maidservant . . ."*

(*Shemos* 21:7). Which is followed by "*When two men fight and harm a pregnant woman* . . . (*Shemos* 21:22), and "*If an ox gores a man*" (*Shemos* 21:28).

You will notice that the subjects that are discussed in the four orders: *Seder Zera'im, Mo'eid, Nashim* and *Nezikin*, are all included in the Book of *Shemos*.

After discussing the laws of the Book of *Shemos*, he goes on outlining the contents of the Book of *Vayikra*. Therefore, *Nezikin* is followed by *Kodashim*. *Kodashim*, the laws of offerings, precedes *Taharos*, the laws of ritual purity. This too, is consistent with the order of the verses. For the Torah lists the laws of sacrifices ahead of the laws of ritual purity and impurity; the laws of sacrifices are in the beginning of *Vayikra*, whereas the laws of purity start only in *parashas Shemini* (*Vayikra*, chapter 11).

The Order and List of the Masechtos

When Rabbi Yehudah HaNasi compiled these six sections, he subdivided each section of general topics into separate parts. Each of these parts he called a *masechta*. These *masechtos* he then split up into chapters, each dealing with a single concept. He called each chapter a *perek*.

He then divided each *perek* into small paragraphs that are simple to understand and easy to memorize and teach to others. He called each paragraph a *halachah* [or *Mishnah*].

I. Seder Zera'im—Agricultural Produce

1) *Maseches Berachos*—Blessings

He began with *maseches Berachos* for a very logical reason. A good doctor who wants to keep a person's health intact will begin by prescribing a balanced diet. With this in mind, Rabbi Yehudah HaNasi began with *Berachos*, because you may not eat anything unless you first say a *berachah*. By assigning first place to *maseches Berachos* he wanted to make a meaningful improvement in the food by introducing a spiritual component into it.

However, in order to keep a unified theme, he included the laws of all *berachos*, those you say over food as well as those you say before performing a mitzvah.

There is only one Biblical mitzvah you have to do each and every day and that is the mitzvah of *Kerias Shema*[1]. Now, it would not be right to discuss the *berachos* of *Kerias Shema* unless you first reviewed the laws of *Kerias Shema* itself. That is why he began *maseches Berachos* with the words, *"Mei'eimasai korin es Shema-* From what time in the evening may you recite the *Shema*?"* and spoke about all other aspects of the *Shema*. He then went on to discuss the laws of the other *berachos* and finally those you say over food.

He then returned to the topic of agriculture.

2) *Pei'ah*—Edge of the Field[2] (*Vayikra* 19:9)

Maseches Pei'ah is the first *Masechta* to follow *Berachos* because it is the only gift of produce a farmer must

---

1. Kerias Shema-the obligation to recite the *"Shema Yisrael"* in the morning and evening.
2. A farmer must leave a portion at the edge of his field for the poor.

make while the standing grain is still rooted in the earth.

3) *Demai*—Questionable Produce[3]

After *Pei'ah* comes *Demai* because the poor may use *demai* just as they use *pei'ah*, as it says, "We let the poor eat *demai*" (*Demai* 3:1).

4) *Kilayim*—Mixture of Seeds

After *Demai* comes *Kilayim*, in line with the order of the verses in *parashas Kedoshim*, where it first says, "*Do not completely harvest the ends of your fields*" (*Vayikra* 19:9), and afterwards, "*Do not plant your field with different species of seeds*" (*Vayikra* 19:19).

5) *Shevi'is*—Sabbatical Year

After *Kilayim* comes *Shevi'is*. By rights, Rabbi Yehudah HaNasi should have placed *Maseches Orlah* after *Kilayim* because that is the order in which they appear in the Torah. But he realized that *orlah* is not a mitzvah that every farmer must observe (as long as he does not plant a tree, the prohibition of *orlah* does not apply to him), and *shevi'is* is a mitzvah everyone must observe. Furthermore, the Torah devotes an entire *sidrah* to *shemittah* (the sabbatical year) which is the subject of *maseches Shevi'is*. Therefore, he placed *Shevi'is* before *Orlah*.

6) *Terumah*—Offering of Produce to the *Kohein*[4]

After *Shevi'is* comes *Terumah*, because the *terumah*

---

3. Since some unlearned people did not set aside the required tithes of their produce, all produce bought from such people was called *demai* [questionable] and had to be tithed before eating it. This rule did not apply to the poor.
4. The first offering to be set aside of the grain produce is the *terumah* which must be given to the *kohen* (*Devarim* 18:4 and *Bamidbar* 18:8)

offering is the first gift that is offered from the grain.

7) *Ma'aseros*—Tithes

After *Terumah* comes *Ma'aseros* which deals with *ma'aseir rishon* [the first tithe—the annual offering given to the *levi'im* (*Bamidbar* 18:21,24), because it is set aside after the *terumah*.

8) *Ma'aseir Sheini*—Second Tithe[5]

After *ma'aseir rishon* [first tithe], he discusses *ma'aseir sheini* [second tithe] which is given after *Ma'aseir Rishon*.

9) *Challah*—Dough Offering[6]

This is followed by *maseches Challah*, because after a person has given all the above mentioned offerings.[*terumah, ma'aseir rishon* and *ma'aseir sheini*]—he grinds the grain into flour and kneads the flour into dough. At that point, *challah* must be separated from the dough.

10) *Orlah*—Prohibited Fruit[7]

After he finishes discussing the laws of the offerings that are given from the grain, he begins to speak about fruits. And so he arranged the *masechtos Orlah* after *Challah*.

---

5. In the first, second, fourth and fifth year of a six year cycle, a second tithe, called ma'aseir sheini had to be set aside. This produce had to be eaten in Yerushalayim, or its equivalent in money had to be spent on food and eaten in Yerushalayim (*Devarim* 14:28,29)
6. The dough offering given to the *kohanim, Bamidbar* 15:17-21
7. The fruit of a tree may not be eaten for the first three years; such fruit is called orlah (*Vayikra* 19:23)

11) *Bikkurim*—First-Fruit[8]

Bikkurim follows *Orlah* in accordance with their sequence in the Torah: The laws of *orlah* are discussed in *Vayikra* 19:23, and the laws of *bikkurim* are described in *Devarim* 26:1-11.

Thus, *Seder Zera'im* consists of a total of eleven *masechtos*.

II. Seder Mo'eid—Festivals

1) *Shabbos*

He began with *maseches Shabbos* because it outranks the Festivals in its holiness, and because it occurs regularly every week. Furthermore, the chapter in the Torah outlining the Festivals begins with Shabbos (*Vayikra* 23:3).

2) *Eiruvin*—Combining Domains[9]

After *maseches Shabbos* he placed *maseches Eiruvin* since the subject matter has to do with Shabbos.

3) *Pesachim*—Pesach

The next *masechta* is *Pesachim* [dealing with the laws of *Pesach*], which is the first mitzvah given through Moshe *(Shemos 12)*. It is also the mitzvah that follows

---

8. The first fruits *(bikkurim)* of the seven species mentioned in *Devarim* 8:8 must be brought to the Beis Hamikdash and presented to the *kohanim* in a festive ceremony that is described in *Devarim* 26:1-11
9. On Shabbos you are forbidden to carry from a private domain into a public domain and vice versa. Private homes in a common courtyard may be combined by means of an *eiruv*, enabling the residents to carry from one house to another.

after Shabbos in the Torah chapter of the Festivals (*Vayikra* 23).

4) *Shekalim*—Shekels[10]

Then comes *Shekalim*, in line with the order in which it appears in the Torah in *Parshas Ki Sisa* (*Shemos* 20:12).

5) *Yoma—Yom Kippur*

Shekalim is followed by *Yoma* [in keeping with the order in the Torah], where the topic of Yom Kippur is elaborated on in *Parshas Acharei Mos*.

6) *Sukkah*—Sukkos

Rabbi Yehudah HaNasi wanted to end his discussion of the *Shalosh Regalim* [the Three Pilgrimage Festivals]. Since he had already discussed the laws of *Pesach*, there remained *Shavuos* and *Sukkos* to be dealt with. However, there are no obligations that are unique to Shavuos. All the things he had to say about *Shavuos* applied to *all* Festivals. Therefore, after *maseches Yoma* he would have placed *Beitzah* which deals with the general laws of Yom Tov. But because there are so many special mitzvos connected with *Sukkos*, he set *Sukkah* before *Beitzah*.

7) *Beitzah*—Laws of Yom Tov

8) *Rosh Hashanah*

At this point, the only Yom Tov listed in the Torah still to be discussed was Rosh Hashanah, and so, after

---

10. The obligation upon each person to donate a half *shekel* [coin] to the *Beis Hamikdash* each year, which was used to buy communal sacrifices

Beitzah, he took up *Rosh Hashanah*.

9) *Ta'anis*—Fasts
After he finished speaking about the Festivals listed in the Torah, he turned to the fasts instituted by the prophets which are mentioned in the Prophets. Therefore, after Rosh Hashanah he placed *maseches Ta'anis*.

10) *Megillah*—Laws of Purim
Next came *maseches Megillah*, because the reading of the *Megillah* was instituted by prophets who lived after those that instituted the fast days.

11) *Mo'eid Katan*—Intermediate Days
After *Megillah* comes *Mo'eid Katan*, which deals with the laws of *Chol Hamo'eid* [the intermediate days of *Pesach* and *Sukkos*], because *Megillah* and *Mo'eid Katan* have one common feature: both on Purim and *Chol Hamo'eid* it is forbidden to fast or eulogize.

12) *Chagigah*—Festival Offering
After he completed the subject of the *Yamim Tovim* and the things you must do on them and everything related to them, he closed the discussion with *maseches Chagigah* which deals with a special obligation related to the *Shalosh Regalim*, [the Three Pilgrim Festivals], namely, to come to the Beis Hamikdash with an offering *(Devarim 16:16)*. He left this topic over for the end, because it does not apply to everyone—only to the men—as it says, *"Three times each year, every male among you must appear before Hashem"* (*Shemos* 23:17).

Thus *Seder Mo'eid* consists of a total of twelve *masechtos*.

III. Seder Nashim—Women

1) Yevamos—Levirate Marriages[11]

He then subdivided *Seder Nashim*, beginning with *maseches Yevamos*. It would have been more sensible to start with *maseches Kesuvos*, since it deals with marriage contracts. However, Rabbi Yehudah HaNasi was prompted by the following consideration: Marriage is a voluntary act, and the *Beis Din* has no power to force a man into marriage. However, the Beis Din does have the power to tell a man, "Either perform *yibbum* and marry your late brother's wife or perform the *chalitzah* ceremony." Thinking that it is right and proper to place laws that are enforceable ahead of laws that are not, he began with *maseches Yevamos*.

2) Kesuvos—Marriage Contracts

He then placed *Kesuvos* next in order.

3) Nedarim—Vows

After *Kesuvos* comes *Nedarim*. The chapter in the Torah dealing with vows and the Talmudic debates about it concentrate on vows made by women, as it says, *"These are the rules that Hashem commanded Moshe regarding the relationship between a man and his wife, and between a father and his daughter"* (*Bamidbar* 30:17). Also when a woman is legally married her husband has the right to annul her vows. That is why *maseches Nedarim* was placed after *Kesuvos*.

---

11. Levirate marriages or *Yibbum*, the law described in *Devarim* 25:5-10 where it is stated that a man must marry his deceased brother's wife if he is childless. If he does not wish to take his sister-in-law as a wife, the *chalitzah* ceremony is performed, whereupon she is free to marry another man.

4) *Nazir*—Nazirite[12]

After *Nedarim* he placed *Nazir*, because a nazir also takes a vow, and when a woman takes a nazirite vow, her husband can nullify her vow. Therefore, after *Nedarim* comes *Nazir*.

5) *Gittin*—Divorce Law

After completing the discussion of the laws of marriage and the related subject of annulling vows, he began the topic of divorce, placing *Gittin*, after *Nazir*.

6) *Sotah*—The Suspected Adulteress

After *Gittin* he recorded *Sotah*, because it is related to the subject of divorce. If a wife commits adultery, the husband and the wife are forced to divorce, as I will explain in my commentary on the Mishnah.

7) *Kiddushin*—Sanctification of the Marriage

After *Sotah* comes *Kiddushin*. You may wonder why *Kiddushin* [the betrothal ceremony] was left for the last, and why it was not placed ahead of *Kesuvos* [which deals with the rights and obligations between husband and wife after their marriage]. The answer is that Rabbi Yehudah HaNasi did not arrange *Kiddushin* before *Kesuvos* so as not to create a separation between *Yevamos* and *Kesuvos* both of which deal with marital relations and should therefore be linked together.

The question remains, Why didn't he at least arrange *Kiddushin* before *Gittin*, and follow the natural sequence of marriage before divorce?

---

12. A person who takes a nazirite vow must abstain from wine or any grape beverage, may not cut his hair, and may not have any contact with the dead.

The reason that he set *Gittin* before *Kiddushin* is that he wanted to follow the pattern of the Torah where divorce is mentioned before marriage:". . .*he shall write her a bill of divorce and place it in her hand* . . .*When she thus leaves his household, she may go and marry another man*" (*Devarim* 24:1-2). From the words "and marry another man" we derive a basic law of *Kiddushin*, as the Talmud explains, "we compare marriage law to divorce law" (*Kiddushin* 5a).

Seder Nashim consists of a total of seven *masechtos*.

IV. Seder Nezikin—Damages

1) Masechta Nezikin
He divided the first *masechta* into three parts:

a. Bava Kamma—[First Gate]
The first part is *Bava Kamma*, which deals with damages caused to property that are classified under the headings of Ox, Pit, Fire, and personal injury. Since the primary duty of the court is to remove the sources of damages, Rabbi Yehudah HaNasi began with *Bava Kamma*.

b. Bava Metzia—[Middle Gate]
After *Bava Kamma* comes *Bava Metzia*, which is concerned with conflicting claims of ownership, law concerning things held in safekeeping, wages, laws concerning borrowing and renting, and everything related to these topics.

He followed the order of the Torah verses; after the laws of damages (Ox, Pit, Fire) (*Shemos* 21:22-33,

22:4-5) and *"when two men fight"* (*Shemos* 21:22), the Torah discusses the laws of the "Four Custodians"[13] (*Shemos* 22:6-14).

c. *Bava Basra*—[Last Gate]

Then comes *Bava Basra*, which deals with laws concerning the division of property held in partnership, adjacent dwellings under co-ownership, cancellations of sales contracts when merchandise is found to be defective, buying and selling, guarantees and hereditary succession.

He made this section the last of the "Three Gates" because its subject matter is based entirely on the Oral Torah and logical reasoning, and is not explicitly mentioned in the Torah.

2) *Sanhedrin*—Judicial Body

Now that we are familiar with the civil laws, Rabbi Yehudah HaNasi deals with the judges who administer these laws. Thus, he arranged *Sanhedrin* after *Bava Basra*.

3) *Makkos*—Flogging

In some editions of the Talmud, *maseches Makkos* [which deals with the punishment of flogging to be administered by the Beis Din], is joined with *maseches Sanhedrin* and is counted as one *masechta* with the explanation that since *Sanhedrin* ends with "The following offenders are to be put to death by strangling," Rabbi Yehudah HaNasi attached to it "The following offenders are to be punished by flogging" [the first

---

13. The Torah distinguishes four categories of custodians, (a) the unpaid custodian, (b) the paid custodian, (c) the borrower, (d) the renter.

words of *maseches Makkos].* This simply is not so. *Makkos* is a *masechta* all by itself. It was placed next to *Sanhedrin* because no one, except the judge, has the right to give a flogging, as it says, ". . .*the judge shall make him lean over and have him flogged (Devarim 25:2).*

4) *Shavuos*—Oaths

Makkos is followed by *Shavuos* because of the similarity of the laws between those at the end of *Makkos* and those at the beginning of *Shavuos*. The Talmud in *Shavuos* comments on this. Another reason for juxtaposing these two *masechtos* is that, similar to flogging, only a judge can compel someone to take an oath.

5) *Eiduyos*—Testimonies

When he completed his discussion of the civil laws, the judges and their powers, such as administering flogging and oaths, Rebbi went on to speak about *Eiduyos* which consists largely of a collection of *halachos* about whose reliability we have the testimony of trustworthy men. We may depend on their testimony. The testimony of witnesses in court is the basis of the judicial system, and these men testified before the *Beis Din* as to the authenticity of these *halachos*. Therefore, it belongs near the laws of *Beis Din*. Rabbi Yehudah HaNasi arranged *Eiduyos* [though it is more closely related to Sanhedrin], after *Shavuos*, whose subject matter is oaths, because people take oaths all the time, whereas *Eiduyos* consists of testimonies that were given to the judges at certain special occasions, and which were then accepted by them.

6) *Avodah Zarah*—Idolatry

Rabbi Yehudah HaNasi then began to discuss the subject of Idolatry, because in order to be qualified, a judge must be thoroughly familiar with the rituals and cults of idol worshippers. When he knows these ceremonies he will be able to apply the law that states that a person who worships the planet Saturn by performing the rites that apply to the planet Venus, or who prays to Jupiter with the prayers of Mars, does not deserve to be put to death, as the Oral Law clearly declares.

He left this *masechta* for the last, because idol worship happens only in extremely rare cases.

7) *Avos*—Ethics of the Fathers

When he finished discussing the requirements of a judge, he began *maseches Avos*, Ethics of the Fathers. He wrote this *masechta* for two reasons.

First, it clearly states that accepted oral tradition is absolutely true and that it was transmitted from generation to generation in an unbroken chain, reaching back to Moshe. You will come to honor the Sage of your generation and treat him with utmost respect, because he is the bearer of the Tradition. It has been transmitted through the ages down to him in his generation, just as the earlier Sages received it in their generation. As we are taught, "If we were to investigate the *Beis Din* of Rabban Gamliel, then we would have to put on trial each *Beis Din* which ever stood, from the days of Moshe until the present" (*Rosh Hashanah* 2:9). "Shimshon was as authoritative in his generation as Shmuel was in his" (*Rosh Hashanah* 25b). There is a important lesson in this for all of us. We should not say, "Why should we accept the decision of This Judge or abide by the ordinance enacted by That Judge?" This attitude is wrong, because the decision was not rendered by the judge alone, but also by Hashem Who said, *"Judgment belongs to G-d"* (*Devarim* 1:17). It is all one and the same system of justice that was transmitted over the ages, from generation to generation.

The second reason for including *maseches Avos* in *Seder Nezikin* is that Rabbi Yehudah HaNasi recorded the ethical sayings of the outstanding Sages, to teach us good character traits. No one needs good character traits more than a judge. If an ignorant person is not a paragon of virtue he does no harm to the community; he only hurts himself. But if a judge is not an ethical and humble man, he will not only hurt himself but also bring harm to the community. Therefore, he begins *maseches Avos* by admonishing the judges, "Be deliberate in judgment" (*Avos* 1:1).

A judge must take to heart all the words of advice that are found in *maseches Avos*, such as to be deliberate in judgment, and not to rush into rendering a verdict, for there may be important aspects that have been withheld by the witnesses; rendering the case a *din merumeh* [suspect to legal trickery or conspiracy] (*Sanhedrin* 32b). On the other hand, he should not draw out the court proceedings unnecessarily, if he knows that there are no suspicious aspects; this would be called *inui hadin* [delaying justice]. He must do his best to interrogate the witnesses thoroughly, and to be careful with his words, and not unwittingly give the witnesses guidance through his line of questioning. Neither should he counsel the litigants on how to plead their case. This is called *orechei hadayanim* [a judge acting as a lawyer]. He should not disgrace himself by associating with ignorant people, for he will lose his dignity. He should not seclude himself, so that people cannot reach him when they need him. He should not pursue leisure and pleasures for in his passion for enjoyment he will lose sight of the truth. He should not want to rank himself higher than his colleagues in the seating order, and he should not make a strong bid for the post of judgeship, for he might be suspected of harboring ulterior motives. He should always try to work out a settlement. If he never in his life rendered a verdict but always reached a settlement, how wonderful that would be. But if a settlement cannot be reached, then he should render a legal decision. He should not be abrupt, but should allow the opposing litigant ample time to plead his case, even if he talks too much and speaks nonsense. If this is impossible, since he cannot see any justification at all in his claim, he should render his decision immediately. We see how our Sages often took immediate decisive action when there was a need for it. The Talmud said about such cases, "Let the law pierce the mountain." (Sanhedrin 6b).

To sum it up, a judge must be like a capable doctor. If he can cure a patient by putting him on a diet he will not prescribe medicine. When he sees that the patient does not respond to the change in the diet he will prescribe natural medicines, like potions, brews and sweet-smelling herbs. Only if he sees that none of these medications have an effect will he prescribe strong bad-tasting medicines like laxatives. Similarly, a judge should begin by trying to reach a settlement. If he cannot, he should pronounce judgment in a quiet way, gently appeasing the losing party. If he cannot appease him because the man is stubborn and insists on winning the case no matter what, then he must become more firm, as it says, *"See every proud man and humble him, and crush the wicked where they stand"* (*Iyov* 40:12).

A judge should not chase after the pleasures of the world, wealth and social status, as it says about judges, *"men . . .who hate improper gain"* (*Shemos* 18:21) and *"A king, by justice sustains the land"* (*Mishlei* 29:4)—"If a judge is like a king who needs nothing, then he sustains the land; but if he behaves like a *kohen* who comes to the threshing floors to collect his *terumah*, then he destroys the land" (*Kesuvos* 105b).

Now that we have seen that a judge needs all these admonitions how perfectly appropriate is it for *masechtes Avos* to be placed after *Sanhedrin*. Once *Avos* contained all this valuable advice to judges, similar wise counsel was added, designed to promote abstention from the empty pleasures of the world, respect for the Sages, integrity and the fear of Heaven.

8) *Horayos*—Erroneous Rulings

When Rabbi Yehudah HaNasi completed the ethical admonitions to the judges, he began to discuss what should be done in case judges render an erroneous decision, for it is impossible for anyone made of flesh and blood not to make mistakes. Therefore, *Horayos* [which deals with erroneous rulings] follows *Avos*, and with it *Seder Nezikin* is ended.

Thus, *Seder Nezikin* comprises eight *masechtos*.

V. *Seder Kodashim*—Sacred Objects

1) *Zevachim*—Animal Offerings

He began *Kodashim* with the animal offerings which form *maseches Zevachim*.

2) *Menachos*—Meal Offerings

After *Zevachim* comes *Menachos* [offerings made of flour] in keeping with the order of these subjects in the Torah (*Vayikra* 1-2).

3) *Chullin*—Non-sacred Meat

Having completed the entire subject of sacrificial offerings, he turned to the laws of slaughtering for non-sacrificial purposes, following the order of the verses. After Hashem said, *"There will be a site that Hashem will choose as the place dedicated to His name. It is there that you will have to bring all that I am prescribing to you.* (*Devarim* 12:11), He said, *"In all your settlements, you may slaughter animals to satisfy your wants, so that you will be able to eat the meat that Hashem gives you as His blessing"* (*Devarim* 12:15). Thus, after *Menachos* comes *Chullin*.

4) *Bechoros*—The First-Born

After *Chullin* comes *Bechoros*, again following the order in which these subjects are mentioned in the Torah. Speaking of non-sacred meat the Torah says, *"In all your settlements, you may slaughter animals to satisfy your wants"* (*Devarim* 12:15). After that it says, *"However, in your settlements, you may not eat the tithes of your grain, wine and oil, the **first-born of your cattle and flocks**, any general pledges you make, your specific pledges, or your hand-delivered elevated gifts"* (*Devarim* 12:17).

5) *Arachin*—Valuations

After discussing the laws regarding things set aside for sacred purposes, he deals with the laws concerning the valuations of objects pledge for sacred purposes. The monetary value of these objects also become sacred. Thus, after *Bechoros*, he arranged *maseches Arachin*

6) *Temurah*—Exchanges[14]

Temurah follows *Arachin* following the order of the Torah verses.

---

14. The Torah states, "One may neither exchange [the animal that was donated] nor offer a substitute for it, whether it be a better animal for a worse one, or a worse animal for a better one. If he replaces one animal with another, both [the original animal] and its replacement shall be consecrated."(*Vayikra* 27:10)

THE STRUCTURE OF THE MISHNAH

7) *Kereisos*[15]

Having completed the discussion of these various offerings, he continues with *maseches Kereisos*, which deals with all transgressions that are punishable by *kares* and related topics. The reason he placed this *masechta* in *Seder Kodashim* [which has to do with offerings] is because every transgression that is punishable by *kares* if done intentionally, requires a sin-offering if it was done inadvertently.

8) *Me'ilah*—Misuse of Sacred Objects[16]

After *Kereisos* he proceeded with *Me'ilah*, because the transgression for which a person must bring a *me'ilah*-guilt offering are less serious than the transgressions for which a sin-offering must be brought.

9) *Tamid*—Daily Offering

After *Me'ilah* comes *maseches Tamid*. He left this *masechta* for the end, because it contains no learned discussions or expositions on things that are forbidden and permitted. Rather, it tells the story of how the daily offering was brought, in order that we will be able to bring it in the future.

10) *Midos*—Measurements

After *Tamid* follows *Midos* which relates a series of facts. It describes the shape and structure of the Beis Hamikdash as well as its measurements. This is useful, for when the Beis Hamikdash will be rebuilt, speedily

---

15. Divine punishment by premature death
16. Which speaks about the offering that has to be brought by a person who used an article that was set aside for sacred purposes, for his own benefit (*Vayikra* 5:15-16)

in our days, we will have to be very careful to build it according to this layout, design and size, since its dimensions were revealed through *ruach hakodesh* [A divine gift of superior understanding, akin to prophecy.], as David said to his son Shlomoh, *"All this that Hashem made me understand by His hand on me, I give you in writing—the plan of [the Beis Hamikdash] all the works"* (*Divrei Hayamim* I 28:19).

11) *Kinim*—Birds

After completing the discussion of animal sacrifices, and the design of the Beis Hamikdash where these sacrifices were offered, he turned to *maseches Kinim*. The only topic discussed in this *masechta* is what should be done if different kinds of bird offerings were mixed up. This subject was left for last because such a mix-up does not necessarily happen. Besides, the discussion is very short, as will be explained.

With this *masechta, Seder Kodashim* is ended. Thus, *Seder Kodashim* contains eleven *masechtos*.

VI. *Seder Teharos*—Ritual Purity

1) *Keilim*—Vessels

He began *Seder Taharos*, with *maseches Keilim*, which concerns the main sources of *tum'ah* [ritual uncleanness], and lists all things that are and are not receptive to *tum'ah*.

2) *Ohalos*—Tents

After *Keilim* comes *Ohalos*, which discusses the *tum'ah* of a dead human being. He assigns first place to this masechta, because the *tum'ah* of a dead body is the most potent source of *tum'ah*.

3) *Nega'im*—Plagues

Following *Ohalos* is *Nega'im*, which deals with the *tum'ah* caused by the disease of *tzora'as* [plague of leprosy], because a person suffering from tzora'as spreads *tum'ah* to everything within the tent or room he occupies. In this respect it has some similarity to the spreading of *tum'ah* by a corpse.

4) *Parah*—Red Cow

After ending the discussion of the *tum'ah* produced by a dead body and of similar *tum'ah*, he goes on to speak about *taharah*, ritual purity, which is attained through the red cow. Therefore, he arranged *masechtas Parah* after *Nega'im*.

5) *Teharos*—Ritual Purity

When he finished the discussion of the more potent sources of *tum'ah* and the process by which ritual purity is attained, he turned to the weaker forms of *tum'ah* which may be ended at sunset by immersing in a *mikveh*. Thus, he placed *masechtas Teharos* after *Parah*. Euphemistically, he named it *Teharos*, substituting that name for the actual subject matter which deals with the weaker forms of *tum'ah*. Another reason for the name *Teharos* is that in order to know the various stages of *tum'ah* you must be familiar with the concept of *taharah*.

Don't think for a moment that giving the name *Teharos* to a *masechta* and giving the same name to the entire *Seder Teharos* was an error on the part of the author. Among philosophers this is not considered an error. They often use the same term for a specific part as for the general concept.

6) *Mikva'os*—Ritual Immersion Pools

After completing the discussion of the more potent and the weaker forms of *tum'ah* and the ways by which ritual cleansing may be attained, he dealt with the specific laws of ritual cleansing. Thus, he arranged *maseches Mikva'os* after *Teharos*.

7) *Niddah*—Menstrual Period

He discussed *Niddah* [dealing with the laws relating to a woman who has a menstrual flow] after all these other forms of *tum'ah*, because it is not a universal *tum'ah*, as it applies only to women. Thus, he placed *Niddah* after *Mikva'os*.

8) *Mach'shirin*—Requirements

Niddah is followed by *Mach'shirin* [which outlines the ways food must be prepared to enable it to become contaminated by *tum'ah*, see *Vayikra* 11:34].

After *Mach'shirin* comes *Zavim*.

9) *Zavim*—Venereal Discharge[17]

Zavim really should have been placed immediately after *Niddah*, but he put *Mach'shirin* ahead of *Zavim*, to conform with the order in which these topics appear in the Torah. The subject of *Mach'shirin* appears in *parashas Shemini* (*Vayikra* 11:34), and the laws of *zavim* are is found in *parashas Metzora* (*Vayikra* chapter 15).

10) *T'vul Yom*—Immersed on that Day[18]

After *Zavim* comes *T'vul Yom*, following the order of the verses, as it says, *"This is the law concerning the man*

---

17. The laws of tum'ah that arise as a result of venereal discharge
18. Detailing the laws of one who has immersed in the *mikveh* and must wait until sunset to become ritually clean, *Vayikra* 22:6-7

who is unclean because of a discharge or seminal emission" (*Vayikra* 15:32).

11) *Yadayim*—Hands

The previous forms of *tum'ah* involved the entire body, in other words, if a person came in contact with these forms of *tum'ah*, his entire body becomes *tamei*. Therefore, Rabbi Yehudah HaNasi now takes up the forms of *tum'ah* that affect only one part of the body, placing *Yadayim* (Hands) after *T'vul Yom*.

12) *Uktzim*-Stems[19]

He left this *masechta* for the last because its laws are derived through reasoning and they are not explicitly mentioned in the Torah. With this *masechta* he closed his work.

Thus, *Seder Teharos* contains a total of twelve *masechtos*.

The total number of *masechtos* in the entire Mishnah adds up to sixty-one. The total number of chapters of all *masechtos* amounts to five hundred and twenty-three.

---

19. The laws concerning the stems of foods in regard to *tum'ah*

Expounding the Mishnah

In compiling the Mishnah, Rabbi Yehudah HaNasi was content to trace the transmission of the Oral Law only as far back as Shimon HaTzaddik. He wrote the Mishnah in a lucid and concise style. To his brilliant mind everything was very clear, but a person of lesser intelligence had difficulty grasping the concepts, since the early Sages wrote on their own level of comprehension. Because of this, Rabbi Chiya, one of Rabbi Yehudah's students, wrote a book patterned after his master's work in which he explained the things that might be puzzling. This is the *Tosefta* [Supplement]. Its purpose is to explain the Mishnah and to provide insights that could not be discovered without a great deal of diligent study. He presented these insights in order to teach us how to derive and develop concepts from the Mishnah.

Rabbi Hoshiah wrote similar works, and so did Rav, who wrote the braisos—[literally, "outside texts"— teaching not found in the Mishna], the *Sifra* [a commentary on *Vayikra*], and *Sifrei* [a commentary on *Bamidbar* and *Devarim*]. There were many other Sages who wrote similar works, as it says in the Talmud, "When a Rabbi came, he brought a *baraisa* with him."

However, none of these *baraisos* matched the Mishnah in the smooth flow of language, clarity and brevity. The Mishnah became the accepted text, and all the other works ranked second to it. The Mishnah was preferred and admired by everyone. [In comparison to other texts], its praise could be summed up in the verse, *"Maidens see her and acclaim her; queens and concubines, and praise her"* (*Shir Hashirim* 6:9).

All those who came after the time of the Mishnah, devoted their energies to nothing but the study of the Mishnah. Generation after generation researched, analyzed and expounded the Mishnah, each scholar according to his wisdom and understanding. With the passing years, differences of opinion arose about the interpretation of some laws. Whenever scholars studied together, invariably they probed and delved into the Mishnah, discovered new insights and increased their knowledge in general. This process of research and analysis continued up to the time of Ravina and Rav Ashi, the last of the Talmudic Sages.

The *Gemara*

Rav Ashi (353—427 C.E.) set himself the task of compiling the *Gemara* [Talmud]. He followed the example of Rabbeinu Hakadosh [Rabbi Yehudah HaNasi] who had collected all the statements of those who came after Moshe. He too gathered all the sayings of the Sages who followed Rabbeinu Hakadosh, including all the explanations of the commentators and the fine legal points they made. He compiled them, digested them with his G-d-given intellect, and composed the *Gemara*. He had four goals in mind:

The First, to explain the Mishnah by a) showing the various interpretations of its text, b) showing the reasoning of the contending sages, c) and revealing which line of reasoning holds true. This was his main purpose.

The Second, to set down the final *halacha* according to one of the sages, whether concerning the text or the meaning of the Mishnah, or about new laws that were derived from the Mishnah.

The Third, to put on record new applications of the law which the Sages of each generation derived from the Mishnah, including the principles and proofs on which the teachers of the Mishnah based their statements, and arranged them in their present form. And to record the preventive measures (*gezeiros*) and enactments that were instituted from Rabbi Yehudah HaNasi's days until his day.

The Fourth, to write down the *Aggadic derashos* [homilies], that fit the theme of the chapter where they are found.

Aggadic Derashos

The Aggadic *derashos* are not to be taken lightly. On the contrary, one should view them seriously, because they are full of great wisdom, amazing secrets and precious treasures. If you look at these *derashos* from an intellectual perspective you will discover in them the supreme, essential good. These *derashos* contain ideas about G-d and the essential good which the mystics keep hidden and do not want to reveal. They also contain all the ideas that the philosophers dealt with. Yet, on the surface they seem to be utter nonsense.

The Sages had very good reasons for disguising these lofty ideas. In the first place, they wanted to sharpen their students' wits and broaden their minds. Also, they wanted to pull the wool over the eyes of the fools, who would not be able to grasp their real meaning. If the fools would be shown the splendor of these truths, in their ignorance they would ridicule them. The Talmud says about these fools, "Do not reveal the secret to them" (*Kiddushin* 71a), since they do not have enough intelligence to grasp the mystical truth.

Even to one another the Sages did not want to reveal the mysteries of Kabbalistic wisdom. The Talmud speaks about this, "One of the Sages got together with some people who were well-versed in the knowledge of *Ma'aseh Bereishis* [the Kabbalistic study of Creation]. He himself was an expert on *Ma'aseh Merkavah* [the mystical description of the Divine Chariot in *Yechezkel, chapter 1*]. He said to them, 'You teach me *Ma'aseh Bereishis* and I will teach you *Ma'aseh Merkavah*.' They agreed. However, after they taught him *Ma'aseh Bereishis*, he refused to teach them *Ma'aseh Merkavah*."

Now, this man certainly did not do this because he was not generous with his scholarship, nor because he wanted to pride himself that he knew more than they did. Heaven forbid! Even fools do not stoop that low, let alone such a respected and pious man. He did this because he thought that he was qualified to understand what they knew, but that they were not capable of grasping what he knew. He found a verse to support his view, *"Honey and milk are under your tongue"*

(*Shir Hashirim* 4:11), meaning, those sweet sciences for which the soul craves like the palate craves honey and milk, must be kept hidden, should not be talked about, and should not even be mentioned or hinted at. That is why it says, "**under** your tongue"—these topics should not be studied and meditated on in public. These secrets are alluded to in the text of the Talmud; and when Hashem will see fit to lift the veil of ignorance from a person's heart, then, if he makes a strong effort and familiarizes himself with the secrets of Kabbalah, he will understand as much as his intelligence can absorb. Having made a sincere effort, there is nothing left for him to do, other than to leave the matter in the hand of the Creator. He should pray to Him and beg Him that He may enlighten him and reveal to him the mysteries that are hidden in the Holy Books. David did this when he said, "*Open my eyes, that I may perceive the wonders of Your teaching*" (*Tehillim* 119:18).

When Hashem opens a man's eyes and reveals to him some of these mystical secrets, he must hide them from others, as we have said. And if he does hint at it ever so slightly, he should do so only to someone who has a brilliant mind and who is known for his integrity, as has been illustrated in many stories in the Talmud. A scholar should reveal his Kabbalistic knowledge only to someone who is more learned than he is, or at least his equal. If he revealed it to a fool, the fool may not disparage him, but he certainly will not appreciate it. *Shlomoh* said about this, "*Do not speak to a fool, for he will disdain your sensible words*" (*Mishlei* 23:9).

A third reason the Sages wrote their *derashos* in the form of symbolism was to teach the masses through allegories and parables. Women, young boys and children will enjoy the stories, and when their intellect has ripened, they will understand the lofty ideas that are at the heart of these stories. Shlomoh hinted at this when he said, *"For understanding proverb and parable, the words of the wise and their allusions"* (*Mishlei* 1:6).

If you come across a parable and you can not grasp its simple meaning, you should be pained by this fact. Don't blame the *derash*, blame your weak mind that is far removed from understanding the basic truth. For it is a fact that some people are smarter than others which is due to differences in their physical makeup. Just as one man may be stronger than another, so is one man's brainpower greater than someone else's. Secondly, even one who is naturally very smart will fail to comprehend many things if he is ignorant of knowledge. The understanding of a man who developed his intellect to understand an intricate matter is definitely greater than that of one who has not developed his intellect. The one who has worked to develop himself has what is called "actual brainpower," while the one who has not worked, has "potential brainpower." Because of that, some people clearly see the truth of certain things, while others find these things to be far-fetched and even impossible. It depends on their intelligence and on how they have developed.

Let me give you an illustration. Think of a man who is a physician, well-versed in arithmetic, a scholar of music, a physicist, and an all around bright fellow, but who knows nothing about geometry and astronomy. Suppose we were to ask his opinion of a man who claimed that the sun which we see as a small disk is really a large sphere, that this sphere is $166^{3}/_{8}$ times as large as the earth, that the earth's sphere has a circumference of 24,000 miles, and that by this method the circumference of the sun can be calculated. No doubt, our bright scientist will be unable to accept such a theory. To him it will sound outlandish and utterly baffling. He will argue immediately that these claims make no sense at all, for how can a man who takes up only a few inches of space on earth know the size of the sun as if it were a piece of real estate? He will exclaim, "How is this possible? Look, the sun in heaven is very far away. We cannot even clearly see the outline of the sun; all we can see is its glow. So how can anyone go up there to survey it and measure it, down to a fraction of 3/8th? This is nothing but absolute nonsense." He will have no doubt at all that these claims are baseless and absurd.

But if he would study geometry and learn the basic theorems of the proportions of spheres and other geometrical shapes, and he would then study the authoritative text on this subject, namely *Almagesti* [written by Ptolemy], the famous work on the calculations of the heavenly orbits, then he would clearly understand this claim, and he will realize that it is undeniably true and can be proven. He will accept the dimensions of the sun, just as he is convinced that the sun exists. He will adjust his mind to believing firmly all the things that he considered incredible earlier. A scenario like this could very well happen. We did not ask a man who is ignorant about science the question, but one who is intelligent, good-natured and wise. The person we asked was familiar with mathematics, a science with its thought process similar to theology. Certainly, if a man who has no common sense and knows nothing about science, a man whose brainpower has not developed, were asked about divine ideas that are hidden in the allegories of the *derashos*, he surely would find them hopelessly unbelievable and would not understand one word of them.

Therefore, we should make allowances for these *derashos*, and analyze them carefully. Let us not be quick to dismiss even one word in them; and when something strikes us as bizarre, let us study the various intellectual sciences, until we understand the concepts that are involved. Even the Sages, although they were eager to study diligently, had brilliant minds, studied in the company of great scholars and kept away from worldly things, still would consider themselves inferior in comparison to earlier sages. They said about themselves, "The wisdom of the early sages was as wide as the entrance to the hall of the *Beis Hamikdash*, and that of the later sages is not even as wide as the eye of a needle" (*Eiruvin* 53a). This certainly applies to us—we have no wisdom at all, as Hashem told us, *"The wisdom of the wise men shall fail, and the prudence of the prudent shall vanish"* (*Yeshayah* 29:14). The prophet Yeshaya in this chapter identifies four negative qualities in us: 1) weak intelligence, 2) a strong appetite for pleasure, 3) laziness in the search for wisdom, and 4) greediness. With these four bad character traits, how can we *not* feel inferior when we compare ourselves to the early sages?

Because the later sages were aware of the fact that all the words of the earlier sages were clear, pure and perfect, they warned us not to ridicule them. They said, "Whoever makes fun of the words of the sages, is sentenced to boiling excrements" (*Gittin* 57a). And there is no greater boiling excrement than the foolishness that makes one belittle the words of the sages. Only a dull-witted, pleasure-seeking sensualist, will dismiss their words.

Because they saw the truth of the early rabbis' words, they devoted their entire lives to studying the Torah and commanded us to immerse ourselves in it at night and part of the day. They considered the study of Torah the height of wisdom, and so it is.

Model of a Derashah

The Sages said, "The Holy One Blessed is He has nothing in this world except for the four cubits of *Halachah*" (*Berachos* 8a). Now, pay close attention to this statement. For if you take it at face value you will find that it appears untrue—as if the four cubits of *Halachah* were the only worthwhile pursuit, and all other sciences were worthless. And furthermore, if this were so, from the days of *Shem* and *Eiver* and onwards until the giving of the Torah, can we say that Hashem had nothing to concern Himself with in this world?

However, if you think about this statement you will find that it contains a marvelous and profound idea. I will explain it to you, so that it may serve as a model for any other *derashos* you may come across. So, please pay close attention.

The Purpose of Existence

The ancient philosophers, after delving deeply into the problem of existence, came to the conclusion that every existing thing needs to have a purpose for which it came into being. Things do not exist without a purpose. Once they established this general rule, they began to sort out all existing things in order to find out the purpose of each object. They discovered that the purpose of every man-made object is known and needs no investigation, for a craftsman will not make an object unless he has a certain purpose in mind. For example, a carpenter would not have made a saw unless he first wondered how to cut a piece of wood, imagined the shape of a saw and began to make it in order to cut wood with it. So we know that the purpose of a saw is to cut wood, the purpose of an ax is to chop, the purpose of a needle is to sew, and so it is with all man-made objects.

But when it comes to things that were created by the divine wisdom through nature, such as trees, herbs, minerals, different rock formations and various kinds of animals, the purpose of some of these are readily apparent, others are not apparent without careful observation and study, while the purpose of others cannot possibly be known unless it is revealed through prophecy or through the power of knowledge of the future.

It is beyond man's ability to explore the reason why some ants have wings and others do not, or why some worms have many legs and others have few, and what is the purpose of a particular species of worm or ant.

However, in regards to larger things whose functions are more obvious it is possible for wise men to argue the purpose of their creation. The wiser a man is, and the greater his hunger and motivation for learning, the more perfect will be his knowledge.

When Hashem granted Shlomoh the wisdom He had promised him, he understood whatever mortal man could possibly comprehend of the secrets of the creation of all species. He spoke about the purpose of the creation of trees, herbs and animals, as it says, *"He spoke about trees, from the cedar in the Lebanon to the moss that grows out of the wall; and he spoke about the beasts, birds, creeping things and fishes"* (*Melachim* I 5:3). This was proof that he had the Divine Spirit. Then it says, *"Men of all peoples came to hear Shlomoh's wisdom"* (*Melachim* I 5:14).

Man Is the Purpose

You should understand that all things that exist beneath the orbit of the moon were created only for the sake of man. Some of the animals are meant to be eaten, like sheep and cattle and other species. Some are here to serve purposes other than nourishment, like a donkey which is meant to carry heavy burdens, or horses which are meant to help man reach distant places in a short time. The benefit of some species we do not know; they do have benefits, though, but we are not aware of what these benefits are. In the same way, some trees, plants and herbs can be eaten, others are used as medicines.

Now, if you find animals or plants that you think cannot be eaten and seem to have no purpose, you should blame it on your lack of knowledge. It is impossible for any herb, fruit or animal—from the elephant to the worm—not to be beneficial for man. Proof of this is that in each generation, extremely beneficial herbs and fruits are discovered that were unknown to earlier generations. The human mind cannot grasp the advantages of each plant, but their benefits will become known through scientific experiments in time to come.

Now you may ask, "For what purpose were deadly poisons created, such as the herb called *beish* or blood herb, which kills people and which has no benefit at all?"

Even these specimens have benefits. For although one dies when eating them, they are not lethal when they are used as an ointment on the body. You should realize that if the venoms of rattlesnakes and viper have great medicinal value, surely things that are less harmful must also carry great benefits.

Man's Purpose Is to Think

Now that we have stated that the purpose of all things is to benefit man, we must also probe the question as to why and for what purpose was man created? After a long investigation, the philosophers concluded that man has a great many functions, in contrast to all species of animals and trees which have only one or two functions. For example, a palm tree has only one function: to produce dates. The same goes for all other trees. Similarly, some animals will be able to spin, like the spider, others will be able to build, like the swallow which builds intricate nests during the summer. Lions can pounce and attack. But man does many different things. They analyzed each of his functions, in order to discover the purpose for which man was created, and they found that his main purpose is to perform one function only. It is for the sake of this one function that he was created, and all his other functions only serve to keep him alive so that he can fulfill his main function. This function is: To form abstract ideas and to know the essential truths. Logic tells you that it is wrong and incorrect to think that the purpose of man's life is to eat, drink and to pursue physical pleasures, or to build a stronghold, because all these activities are passing, short-lived events; they do not improve his inner worth, and besides, all other creatures do the same things. On the other hand, wisdom does add to his inner being and lifts him from disgrace to esteem. Originally he was only a potential man but wisdom made him an actual man. Before developing his knowledge, a man is no better than a beast, for the only thing that makes him different than other living creatures is his ability to think logically and form abstract ideas. Now, the loftiest idea a man can think of is the Unity of Hashem and all theological concepts that flow from this. All other fields of study are only exercises by which to train your mind until it reaches knowledge of Hashem. A full discussion of this subject would take up too much space.

As you attain understanding of these lofty thoughts, you must learn to stay away from most sensual pleasures. It is a fundamental rule that your soul suffers when you indulge your body, and your soul is restored when you restrain your body. A person who chases after bodily pleasures and lets his intellect be dominated by his feelings becomes like an animal that can only think of eating, drinking and mating; such a person loses his G-d-given power to think abstract thoughts. He will turn into a vulgar creature, roaming around in a sea of emptiness.

We have made it clear that the purpose of the world and all that is in it is the wise and good man, the person who understands that wisdom and deeds are what make him a man. By "wisdom" I mean the ability to see the truth as it really is, and to understand whatever man can understand. By "deeds" I mean refining and curbing your innate tendencies, not to be swept along by sensual desires, but enjoying only those things that will benefit your physical, mental and spiritual health. A man who lives according to these notions is the ideal and accomplished man.

We have heard this not only from the prophets, but even the scholars of the various nations, men who have never seen a prophet or heard his wisdom- even they knew that a man is not perfect unless he represents "wisdom and deeds." It will be enough if I just quote the words of the famous philosopher [Aristotle] who said, "G-d demands of us that we are wise and upright men." If a man is supposedly wise and righteous but runs after worldly delights, that man is not really a wise man. Wisdom demands that a person should enjoy luxuries only if they are good for his health. (In our commentary on *maseches Avos* we will give this theme the full attention it deserves).

Along similar lines, we find that the prophet reprimands a person who boasts that he is wise, yet rebels against the mitzvos, and seeks hedonistic pleasures, *"How can you say, 'We are wise, and we possess Hashem's Torah?'. . . See, they reject the word of Hashem, so their wisdom amounts to nothing"* (*Yirmiyah* 8:8-9).

On the other hand, if a man serves Hashem, abstains from enjoyment—except for that which he needs for his health—lives a life of moderation, has the best character traits—but does not possess wisdom, he is not perfect either. But he certainly is better than the first person we discussed; only, his deeds don't have proper direction, and are not performed truthfully. The Sages said about such a person, "A boor cannot be fearful of sin, an unlearned person cannot be scrupulously pious" (*Avos* 2:6). Anyone who says about an ignorant man that he is pious, denies simple logic and contradicts the sages who made a clear cut statement about this. Indeed, the Torah always mentions first the command, *"you should study [the mitzvos],"* and only afterwards is says, *"You should keep them"* (*Devarim* 5:1). Learning is mentioned before doing, because knowledge helps you to do things the right way, but by doing you do not increase your knowledge. The Sages put it this way, "Learning leads to doing" (*Kiddushin* 40b).

Purpose of the Unlearned

There is still one problem: You may ask, "You have just told me that divine wisdom does not create anything useless, everything has a purpose. You also said that man is the preeminent creature, and was created for the purpose of conceiving thoughts and ideas. Now, if that is the case, why did Hashem call into being all those people who cannot form a creative thought? We see that most people are dense and empty-headed, seeking only worldly pleasures, while there are only very few outstanding wise men who reject material values. In fact, you may find no more than one wise man in several generations.

Those ignorant people were created for two reasons: The first reason is to attend to the needs of that one wise man. If all human beings were thinkers and philosophers the world economy would be destroyed and the human race would perish within a short time. Man is basically a helpless creature who needs many services. The wise man would have to learn how to plow, harvest, thresh, grind and bake, and to make the necessary tools for all this work in order to prepare his food. He would have to learn how to spin and weave in order to make clothing. Then he would have learn how to build a place to live, and fashion the tools for all these jobs. Even if he lived as long as *Mesushelach* he would not have enough time to learn all the trades that are essential for him to survive. When would he find time to study and acquire wisdom? Therefore, the rest of mankind was created to provide all the services of a smooth-running society so that the scholar's needs are met, the nation's economy will function well, and scholarship will flourish. How apt is the saying, "If it were not for the foolish the world would lay in ruin." The fool referred to here, is the folly of an ordinary man. He has a weak constitution, yet he travels from one end of the world to other, crossing oceans during the winter, traveling through dry desert land in the scorching heat of summer, risking his life by exposing himself to wild animals and snakes, in order to earn a few dollars. And when he accumulates some money for which he jeopardized his life, he will pay it out to laborers to build a foundation deep in the earth, made of cement and stones, in order to erect on it a stronghold that will stand for many years, although he knows full well that there are not enough years left in his life to outlast a building made of reeds. Can there be a greater foolishness and idiocy than this? By the same token, all worldly pleasures are madness and insanity; still they are needed to keep the world going. This is why the Sages called an ignorant person an *am ha'aretz* [a "person of the land"], meaning that he was created just to keep the land going.

Someone may argue, "Do we not find at times a fool, who enjoys life and does not work hard, while others serve him and take care of his business?; and it might very well be that a wise man is taking care of his business!"

Things are not the way they look on the surface. The pleasure of that imbecile also serves a purpose; it is preparing something good for someone whom the Creator wants to give it to in the future. Because he relaxes and enjoys his money, the imbecile will order his employees to build him a beautiful palace or plant an impressive vineyard, like kings or princes do. It is quite possible that this palace is really being built for a pious man who, one day many years later, will come and find shelter from the scorching sun in the shade of one of its walls. The palace will actually have saved him from death. This thought is expressed in the verse, *"Should he pile up silver like dust, lay up clothing like dirt—he may lay it up, but the righteous will wear it, and the innocent will share his silver"* (*Iyov* 27:17). Or, one day a cup of wine from that vineyard will be used to make a medicine called *tri'aka* which will save the life of a perfectly righteous man who was bitten by a snake. This is Hashem's way and this is His wisdom with which he directs nature, *"for You planned ideas of long ago, fulfilled in steadfast faithfulness (Yeshayah* 25:1).

This concept was taught by the Sages, "When Ben Zoma would stand on the Temple Mount and see Israel coming to celebrate, he would say, 'Blessed is He Who created all these to care for me" (*Berachos* 58b), for he was the greatest sage in his generation.

The second reason for the existence of people who have no wisdom is, that there are only very few wise men. Hashem in His wisdom wanted it that way. You cannot ask why this is so, any more than you can ask why there are nine heavenly spheres, seven planets, and four basic elements, because all these matters and others like them were willed by Hashem when He created the universe. The Sages explained this, "Rabbi Shimon ben Yochai said about his contemporaries, [although they were towering personalities], 'I have seen scholars who have reached eminence, and there are only a few; . . .if there are two, they are myself and my son" (*Sukkah* 45b).

Since there are only very few sages, the masses were created to provide companionship for the sages.

You might think that this is an unimportant benefit; on the contrary, it is essential and even more important than the first. For Hashem Himself settled evil people in *Eretz Yisrael* to provide an pre-existing society for the Children of Israel, and in order to keep the pious ones from being alone, as it says, *"I will not drive them out in a single year, lest the land becomes depopulated . . ." (Shemos 23:29).*

The Sages commented on this idea, in explaining the verse, *"fear God and keep his commandments—because this is all man" (Koheles 12:13).* Literally translated it means, "this" [fearing God and keeping his commandments] is the purpose of all man. The sages interpret it as follows: "because of this" [the perfect man], all man was created.

To sum it up, it has become clear that the goal of Creation was to bring into being the perfect man who possesses both "wisdom" and "good deeds," as we explained.

When you will study and think about what the words of the Sages teach us about these two concepts (wisdom and deeds), then you will see that they were correct when they said, "The Holy One, Blessed is He has nothing in this world except the four cubits of Halachah."[1]

We have strayed a little from our topic, but I brought up these matters because they strengthen the faith, and stimulate a desire for wisdom, and, in my opinion, they are quite important.

Now, let us get back to our subject.

---

1. The Rambam's original question was "How can we say that Hashem has nothing in the world besides the four cubits of Halacha when in fact there exists many sciences in the world other than Halacha? We also find many generations where there wasn't Torah study." His answer appears to be that once we have established that although there are many sciences and unlearned generations, their ultimate purpose is to serve the perfect man. It is correct to say the purpose of the entire world is the perfect man. Since man will not attain perfection without learning Halachah we can properly say that *Hashem has nothing in the world except the four cubits of Halachah.*

Following the Completion of the Talmud

When Rav Ashi completed the compilation of the Talmud as we have it today, the magnificence and the extraordinary usefulness of this work attested to the fact *"that the spirit of G-d was in him"* (*Daniel* 4:5).

Of the sixty-one *masechtos* of the Mishnah, only thirty-five are expounded on in Rav Ashi's work: We find no *Gemara* on *Seder Zera'im*, except for *maseches Berachos*.

There is no Gemara on *Shekalim*, in *Seder Mo'ed*.

There is no Gemara on *Eiduyos* and *Avos*, in *Seder Nezikin*.

There is no Gemara on *Midos* and *Kinim*, in *Seder Kodashim*.

There is no Gemara on any *masechta* in *Seder Tehoros*, except for *Niddah*.

Rav Ashi passed away in Babylonia after he completed the Talmud.[This Talmud is referred to as the Babylonian Talmud.] The Sages of *Eretz Yisrael* did what Rav Ashi had done and composed the Jerusalem Talmud. It was compiled by Rabbi Yochanan.

We find all the *masechtos* of five *sedarim* expounded on in the Jerusalem Talmud. However, no *masechta* of *Seder Teharos* is expounded in the Talmud, neither in the Babylonian nor in the Jerusalem Talmud, except for *Niddah*, as we mentioned. But if you work hard and study diligently at it you can understand this *Seder*, with the help of the *Tosefta* and the *Baraisos*. One can assemble all the relevant laws scattered throughout the Talmud and by a process of analysis deduce the underlying principles and themes of these halachos, as you will see me do when I explain that *Seder*, with G-d's help.

When all the Sages had passed away, the last of whom were Ravina and Rav Ashi, the Talmud was completed and its text firmly established. All sages who came afterwards strived with all their might to understand the recorded text only; no one was permitted either to add to the text or subtract from it.

The *Geonim* wrote many commentaries, but none of them, as far as we know, had the opportunity of completing a commentary on the entire Talmud. Some of them did not live long enough, others were busy settling legal disputes. However, they did compose complete halachic codes, some in Arabic, others in Hebrew, such as *Halachos Gedolos* [Great Laws], *Halachos Ketanos* [Brief Laws], *Halachos Pesukos* [Legal Decisions], Halachos Rav Acha MiShavcha [Decisions of Rav Acha of Shavcha], and others. Then there were the halachos written by the illustrious Rabbi Yitzchak Alfasi. This work is equivalent to all previous works because it includes all the decisions and laws we need in our time of the Exile. In his work, the *Rif* [an acronym for Rabbi Yitzchak Alfasi] clears up all errors in the books of earlier authorities. His work I have found flawless, except for fewer than ten halachos.

However, each of the existing commentaries of the

Geonim has its own merits, according to the author's intelligence. A discerning person who studies the Talmud in depth can judge each gaon's intellectual power by his words and commentaries.

Now that it is our turn, we have done our utmost to research the works of the earlier authorities, and to toil to the utmost of our capabilities, hoping to find favor in the eyes of our Creator. I have collected anything I could lay my hands on from the commentaries of my father, and others, which they received from Rabbi Yosef HaLevi ibn Migash. Rabbi Yosef ibn Migash, a student of the Rif, succeeded him as rabbi of Alusina (Lucene) Spain. The passion this man had for studying the Talmud astonishes anyone who studies his works. The depth of his intellect is such that one could almost say of him, *"There was no king like him before"* (*Melachim* II 23:25) in his method and approach to research. I also assembled whatever I found of his personal notes on the halachos, and whatever I was able to learn from the various commentaries and what I have learned from the various branches of science. I then wrote a commentary on the three *Sedarim*: *Mo'ed, Nashim* and *Nezikin*, except for four *masechtos*. I am planning now to write on them too, but I have not yet found the time to do so. I also wrote a commentary on *Chullin* because there is an urgent need for it.

And that is what I have been working on.

Discussion About the Commentary on the Mishnah

I then decided to write a sorely needed commentary on the *Mishnah*, following the pattern that I will discuss at the end of this chapter.

I was prompted to write this work by the following consideration:

I saw that the *Gemara* tells us things about the Mishnah that you could never deduce through logical analysis. For example, the Gemara will say, "This Mishnah is speaking about a specific circumstance," or, "There are certain words missing in this Mishnah, and it should be amended to read . . . ," or, "This Mishnah is according to so-and-so whose opinion is such. . ." In addition, the Gemara adds words to the mishnah or deletes words from it, and reveals the underlying reason of the Mishnah. By writing this commentary on the Mishnah I hoped to be helpful in four ways:

1) To give a clear interpretation of the Mishnah and explanation of its words. For if you would ask any of the great Sages for an explanation of a law in a mishnah, he could not tell you a thing unless he knew the

Gemara on that mishnah by heart. Or he would tell you, "Let me look up what the Gemara has to say about this." Now, no one can know the entire Gemara by heart, and certainly not when the discussion of that particular law takes up four or five pages in the Gemara. There are so many intricacies, claims, rebuttals, questions and answers, that only an expert in analytical thought can extract a clear cut decision from the Gemara's discussion of the Mishnah. Even such a person will find it difficult when it comes to decisions that are based on knowledge of two or three Masechtos.

2) The second benefit of my commentary is that it will state the final decision. I will clearly tell you according to whose opinion each law was decided.

3) The third advantage is that it will serve as an introduction for any beginner to in-depth Talmudic analysis. He will gather from it an approach of how to reduce a statement to its elements and assess its meaning. With the help of this system the entire Talmud will become like an open book to him.

4) The fourth advantage is that it will help anyone who has mastered the Talmud, to memorize it, so that whatever he has read will be permanently imprinted in his mind, and he will have the Mishnah and the Gemara at his finger tips.

As I imagined such a project, I took courage to carry out my plan. My primary goal is to clarify the Mishnah according to the Gemara's explanation, selecting only valid interpretations, staying away from explanations that the Talmud rejects. I will tell the underlying reasons that led to differences of opinion between the opposing parties, and I will state according to whom the law was decided as it is explained in the Gemara. I will make sure to be brief, in order not to confuse the reader. Our commentary is not meant to teach someone who is obstinate like stone, but to enlighten those who want to understand.

I decided to arrange my work along the lines of all commentators, i.e., I will first copy the words of the mishnah until the end of the law. Then I will discuss the explanation of that law in the way I described. I will then deal with the next law in the same way, and so, until the end of the mishnah. Laws that are well-known and whose meaning need no explanation I will simply write down, and it will not be necessary to comment on it.

Let me point out, that wherever the opinions of *Beis Shammai* and *Beis Hillel* are in conflict, the halachah is decided according to Beis Hillel, with certain exceptions. Only in those cases will I make an exception and state that the halachah follows Beis Shammai.

In the same way, the law is always decided according to an anonymous mishnah in which there is no dispute, except in a few isolated cases. Again, only in those rare cases will I tell you that this anonymous mishnah is rejected and is not the halachah.

It is not necessary to deal at great length with other halachic disputes; I will immediately tell you according to which authority the law is decided. And even in a case where it is one individual's opinion against a majority, I will state that the halachah is decided according to the majority.

May the Almighty show me the way to the truth, and steer me away from untruth.

Written with the help of God Who is uplifted and exalted.

Appendix

I have decided to include in this introduction ten sections relating to the Mishnah. However, they certainly are not quite as important as our primary subject. Still, anyone wishing to know the Mishnah thoroughly would do well to study these sections.

The first section deals with those Sages who are mentioned in the Mishnah, and in whose names the law is quoted.

The second section deals with those Sages who are mentioned in the Mishnah because they played a part in an incident, or because of a moral lesson that can be learned from them, or because of a homiletical explanation they gave to a verse.

The third section offers information about the hereditary status of the Sages in the Mishnah.

The fourth section tells you the chronological order of the Sages and which of the Sages of the Mishnah were contemporaries.

The fifth section identifies the Sages and their disciples.

The sixth section identifies the Sages whose names are vague and undefined.

The seventh section discusses the various titles the author of the Mishnah assigned to the Sages.

The eighth section discusses the various nicknames given to the Sages relating to country, occupation, people or family.

The ninth section discusses the Sages who were involved in most of the disputes in the Mishnah.

The tenth section discusses the number of times a Sage is mentioned in the Mishnah.

Section One

Sages whose laws are quoted in the Mishna. As we have said earlier, the author of the Mishnah began his list of the men involved in transmitting the Oral Law with Shimon HaTzaddik and his colleagues. The total number of sages of the Mishnah whose names are associated with the laws, questions, enactments and preventive measures adds up to ninety-one. They are:

1. Rabbi Eliezer ben Hyrkanos
2. Rabbi Eliezer ben Yaakov
3. Rabbi Eliezer son of Rabbi Yosei Hagelili
4. Rabbi Yehoshua ben Perachyah
5. Rabbi Yehoshua ben Chananiah
6. Rabbi Yehoshua ben Korchah
7. Rabbi Yehoshua ben Beseira
8. Rabbi Yehoshua ben Hyrkanos
9. Rabbi Eliezer ben Azariah
10. Rabbi Elazar ben Yehudah of Bartusa
11. Rabbi Elazar ben Rabbi Tzadok
12. Rabbi Elazar ben Shamua
13. Rabbi Elazar Chasma
14. Rabbi Elazar ben Parta
15. Rabbi Elazar ben Rabbi Shimon
16. Rabbi Elazar ben Pavi
17. Rabbi Yehudah ben Rabbi Ila'i
18. Rabbi Yehudah ben Beseira
19. Rabbi Yehudah ben Bava
20. Rabbi Yehudah ben Abba
21. Rabbi Yehudah ben Tabbai
22. Rabban Shimon ben Gamliel
23. Rabbi Shimon ben Yochai
24. Rabbi Shimon Hashezuri
25. Rabbi Shimon ben Nannas
26. Rabbi Shimon ben HaSegan
27. Shimon ben Shetach
28. Shimon HaTeimani
29. Rabbi Shimon ben Azzai

30. Rabbi Shimon ben Zoma
31. Rabbi Shimon ben Elazar
32. Rabbi Shimon ben Yehudah
33. Rabbi Shimon ben Beseira
34. Shimon achi Azariah
35. Rabbi Chanania Segan HaKohanim
36. Rabbi Chanina ben Antigonus
37. Rabbi Chaninah ben Chachina'i
38. Rabbi Chananiah ben Gamliel
39. Rabbi Nechunia ben Elchanan Ish K'far HaBavli
40. Rabbi Yishmael
41. Rabbi Nechemiah
42. Rabbi Nechemiah Ish K'far HaBavli
43. Rabbi Yochanan ben Nuri
44. Yochanan Kohein Gadol
45. Rabban Yochanan ben Zakkai
46. Rabbi Yochanan ben Beroka
47. Yochanan ben Gudgoda
48. Rabbi Yochanan HaSandler
49. Rabbi Yochanan ben Yashua, son of Rabbi Akiva's father-in- law
50. Rabbi Yosi
51. Rabbi Yosi ben Meshullam
52. Rabbi Yosi ben HaChoteif Efrasi
53. Rabbi Yosi HaGelili
54. Yosef ben Yo'ezer
55. Yosef ben Yochanan
56. Rabbi Yosi ben Rabbi Yehudah
57. Rabbi Yosi HaKohen
58. Yosi ben Choni
59. Rabban Gamliel
60. Rabbi Gamliel HaZaken
61. Dusta'i Ish K'far D'mai
62. Rabbi Dusta'i ben Rabbi Yannai
63. Abba Shaul
64. Rabbi Tarfon
65. Rabbi Meir
66. Rabbi Akiva
67. Rabbi Chutzpis
68. Rabbi Nassan
69. Nachum HaLavlar
70. Rabbi Miyasha

71. Rabbi Tzadok
72. Nachum HaMadi
73. Rabbi Dosa ben Hyrkanos
74. Rabbi Ila'i
75. Rabbi Kuvri
76. Rabbi Pappaias
77. Rabbi Masya ben Cheresh
78. Nitai HaArbeli
79. Shemayah
80. Avtalyon
81. Hillel
83. Shammai
84. Rabbi Zechariah ben HaKatzav
85. Admon
86. Chanan ben Avshalom
87. Rabbi Yadua HaBavli
88. Akavya ben Mehalalel
89. Rabbi Yakim Ish Chadid
90. Menachem ben Chanina'i

We have not listed these names in chronological order.

[This list contains only ninety names instead of ninety-one. The Rambam meant to say that including Rabbi Yehudah HaNasi, the compiler of the Mishnah the number of Sages would total ninety-one.]

Section Two

Sages mentioned in the Mishnah because they played a part in an incident or because of a moral lesson that can be learned from them or because of a homiletic explanation they gave to a verse. Many Sages in the Mishnah are not associated with a law, but they are mentioned because of an incident that happened during their time. Or, because they taught moral lessons like those in *maseches Avos*. The number of Sages mentioned in the Mishnah for these or similar reasons amounts to thirty-seven:

1. Rabbi Yehoshua ben Levi
2. Rabbi Elazar Hakapar
3. Rabbi Elazar ben Arach
4. Rabbi Elazar Hamodai
5. Yehudah ben Teima
6. Rabbi Shimon ben Nesanel
7. Rabbi Shimon ben Akashya
8. Rabbi Shimon ben Chalafta
9. Chanina ben Dosa
10. Chanina ben Chizkiya ben Garon
11. Rabbi Chanania ben Teradyon
12. Rabbi Nechunia ben Hakanah
13. Rabbi Yishmael ben Pavi
14. Yochanan ben Hachoroni
15. Rabbi Yosi ben Rabbi Yehudah Ish K'far HaBavli
16. Rabbi Yosi ben Durmaskis
17. Rabban Gamliel, son of Rabbi Yehudah HaNasi
18. Rabbi Shimon Ish Hamitzpah
19. Choni Hame'ageil
20. Rabbi Hyrkanos
21. Rabbi Yannai
22. Rabbi Nehora'i
23. Antignos Ish Socho
24. Rabbi Chalafta Ish K'far Chanania
25. Rabbi Levitas Ish Yavneh
26. Rabbi Yonasan
27. Shmuel HaKatan
28. Ben Bag Bag
29. Ben Hei Hei
30. Eliho'eini ben Hakaf
31. Chanamel HaMitzri
32. Rabbi Shimon ben Menasia
33. Abba Shaul ben Botnis
34. Zechariah ben Kevutal
35. Bava ben Buta

36. Rabbi Yishmael son of Rabbi Yochanan ben Beroka
37. Rabbi Yishmael ben Rabbi Yosi

Here too, I have not listed the names in chronological order.

Consequently, the total number of Sages mentioned in the Mishnah is one hundred and twenty eight. However, there are two names we have omitted: Elisha *Acher* (the Other), whom we did not count among the virtuous Sages because of his dishonorable conduct which is well-known, and Menachem, mentioned as a colleague of Shammai who was not listed because we found no place for him in any of the classifications we have created.

Section Three

The hereditary status of the Sages of the Mishnah.

The Sages who were of noble birth:
 Rabban Gamliel III, son of
 Rabbi Yehudah HaNasi, son of
 Rabban Shimon III, son of
 Rabban Gamliel II of Yavneh, son of
 Rabban Shimon II, son of
 Rabban Gamliel the Elder, son of
 Rabban Shimon I, son of,
Hillel HaNasi; this is the Hillel of Babylonia who was the leader of the assembly of later Sages who upheld his decisions and who were known as *Beis Hillel*.

Hillel himself was a descendant of Shefatya, son of Avital who was the son of David. Therefore, these seven Sages issuing from Hillel are all descendants of King David.

Four of the Sages mentioned in the Mishnah are converts or descendants of converts to Judaism:
1. Shemayah
2. Avtalyon
3. Rabbi Akiva
4. Rabbi Meir

Some of the Sages were *kohanim*:
1. Shimon HaTzaddik, to whom the entire Oral Law can be traced, in fulfillment of the prophecy concerning *kohanim*, "They shall teach your laws to Jacob" (*Devarim* 33:10).
2. Rabbi Elazar ben Azariah, the tenth generation after Ezra,
3. his uncle, Shimon, known as Shimon achi Azariah.
4. Rabbi Elazar ben Shamua
5. Rabbi Chanania Segan HaKohanim
6. his son, Rabbi Shimon, known as Rabbi Shimon ben HaSegan
7. Yishmael ben Pavi
8. Yochanan Kohen Gadol
9. Rabbi Yochanan ben Zakkai
10. Yosi ben Yoezer
11. Rabbi Yosi HaKohen
12. Rabbi Tarfon
13. Eliho'eini ben Hakaf
14. Chanamel HaMitzri

The rest of the sages were non-kohanim, and as far as I know, were not of prominent ancestry.

Section Four

The chronological order of the Sages in the Mishnah and which of the Sages were contemporaries:

Shimon HaTzaddik and Rabbi Dosa ben Hyrkanos were contemporaries. Rabbi Dosa ben Hyrkanos lived an extremely long life, living into the generation of Rabbi Akiva. These two are known as the First-Generation Group.

The Second Generation Group comprised
  Antignos Ish Socho and
  Rabbi Elazar ben Charsom.

The Third Generation Group comprised
  Yosi ben Yoezer Ish Tzereidah and
  Yosi ben Yochanan Ish Yerushalayim.

The Fourth Generation Group comprised
  Yochanan ben Mattisyah
  Yehoshuah ben Perachyah and
  Nitai Ha'arbeili

The Fifth Generation Group comprised
  Choni HaMe'ageil
  Eliho'eini ben Hakaf
  Yehudah ben Tabbai and
  Shimon ben Shetach.

The Sixth Generation Group comprised
  Akavya ben Mehalalel
  Shemaya
  Avtalyon
  Admon and Chanon
  Rabbi Myasha

The Seventh Generation Group comprised
- Shammai
- Hillel
- Menachem
- Yehudah ben Beseirah
- Rabbi Pappias
- Rabbi Yochanan ben Bag
- Chanania ben Chizkiah ben Garon
- Nechuniah ben Hakanah
- Bava ben Buta
- Rabbi Yochanan ben Hachoroni
- Rabban Gamliel the Elder and
- Nachum HaLavlar

These seven groups spanned the era beginning with the Second *Beis Hamikdash,* until its destruction. None of them saw its destruction.

[The Eighth Generation] witnessed the destruction. They comprised:
- Rabbi Eliezer ben Yaakov
- Rabbi Tzadok
- Rabbi Eliezer, his son
- Rabbi Yochanan ben Zakkai and his students
- Rabbi Yishmael ben Elisha, the Kohen Gadol
- Abba Shaul
- Rabbi Elazar HaModa'i
- Rabbi Chanina Segan HaKohanim
- Rabban Gamliel
- Rabbi Shimon, his son
- Rabbi Chanina ben Antignos
- Rabbi Chanina ben Dosa
- Rabbi Chanina ben Teradyon
- Shmuel Hakatan
- Rabbi Elazar ben Parta
- Rabbi Elazar ben Dama
- Chanania ben Chachina'i
- Rabbi Yehudah ben Abba

[The Ninth Generation which was] the second generation after the Destruction comprised:

Rabbi Tarfon
Rabbi Akiva
Rabbi Elazar ben Azariah
Rabbi Yishmael
Rabbi Yehoshua ben Korcha
Chanania Ish Ono
Shimon ben Nannas
Yochanan ben Baroka
Rabbi Yishmael, his son
Rabbi Yochanan ben Gudgoda
Rabbi Elazar Chasma
Rabbi Yehudah ben Teima

[The Tenth Generation Group which was] the third generation of Tanna'im after the Destruction comprised:
Rabbi Meir
Rabbi Yehudah ben Ila'i
Rabbi Yosi
Rabbi Nassan
Rabbi Yochanan HaSandler
Rabbi Yosi HaGelili
Rabbi Elazar ben Shamua
Shimon ben Azai
Shimon ben Zoma
Rabbi Chutzpis HaMeturgeman

[The Eleventh Generation Group which was] the fourth generation of Tanna'im after the Destruction comprised:
Rabbi Yehudah HaNasi
Rabban Gamliel III
Rabbi Shimon IV
Rabbi Shimon ben Yochai
Rabbi Elazar, his son
Rabbi Shimon ben Elazar
Rabbi Yishmael ben Rabbi Yosi and
Rabbi Yonasan

This group represents the last generation of Sages mentioned in the Mishnah.

Section Five

The Sages and their disciples.

1. In our opening remarks we indicated that Rabbi Yehudah HaNasi, the compiler of the Mishnah, was a disciple of his father. In the same way, each of his predecessors was the student of his father, going back to Hillel and further back to Shimon HaTzaddik.

2. Rabban Yochanan ben Zakkai was also a disciple of Hillel, he had five disciples:
   Rabbi Eliezer ben Hyrkanos
   Rabbi Yehoshua ben Chananiah
   Rabbi Yosi HaKohen
   Rabbi Shimon ben Nesanel and
   Rabbi Elazar ben Arach

This is the group that was assured of life in the World to Come for themselves and their disciples, as it says in the Talmud (*Chagigah* 14).

3. Rabbi Akiva was the disciple of Rabbi Eliezer ben Hyrkanos, his primary teacher. Rabbi Akiva also studied with Rabbi Tarfon for a short time, but as a colleague rather than a student. However, Rabbi Akiva would respect Rabbi Tarfon and address him as "Rabbi," while Rabbi Tarfon would address Rabbi Akiva simply as "Akiva." Rabbi Akiva's esteem of Rabbi Tarfon can be seen in the fact that Rabbi Akiva said, "Allow me to review before you something you have taught me." (*Sifra* 4)

4. Rabbi Meir and Rabbi Shimon ben Yochai were disciples of Rabbi Akiva who was their primary

teacher. Rabbi Meir also studied under Rabbi Yishmael and others (*Eiruvin 13a*).

5. Rabbi Yehudah ben Ila'i studied mainly under Rabbi Elazar ben Azariah.

6. Whenever it says in the Mishnah "This Rabbi said in the name of That Rabbi," it means that the former was a student of the latter, and that is why he received the statement from him.

7. Rabbi Yehudah HaNasi received part of his instruction studying under Rabbi Elazar ben Shamua (*Yevamos* 84a).

8. Sumchus was a disciple of Rabbi Meir. After Rabbi Meir's death, Sumchus planned to study under Rabbi Yehudah, but his plan did not materialize.

Section Six

Sages whose names are vague and undefined.

1. If the Mishnah mentions a Sage simply as "Rabbi Eliezer" without any further identification, it refers to Rabbi Eliezer ben Hyrkanos, a disciple of Rabban Yochanan ben Zakkai.
2. "Rabbi Yehoshua" without any further identification refers to Rabbi Yehoshua ben Chanania, a Student of Rabban Yochanan ben Zakkai.
3. "Rabbi Yehudah" without further qualification refers in the Mishnah to Rabbi Yehudah ben Ila'i. It is he whom the Talmud has in mind when it says, "An

incident happened with a certain *chasid*," for he was known by that title.

4. "Rabbi Elazar" without further identification, refers to Rabbi Elazar ben Shamua HaKohen, who lived in Rabban Gamliel's generation. It was his disciples who refused to allow Rabbi Yehudah HaNasi to give a lecture in their *Beis Midrash* (*Yevamos* 84a).

5. "Rabbi Shimon," simply stated, refers to Rabbi Shimon ben Yochai, a disciple of Rabbi Akiva, whose episode involving a Roman Caesar is well known. [After making a unflattering remark about the Roman government, Rabbi Shimon ben Yocha'i was condemned to death. He hid in a cave for twelve years, emerging only after the Caesar's death (*Shabbos* 33b).]

6. "Rabbi Elazar ben Rabbi Shimon" refers to Rabbi Shimon ben Yocha'i's son (*Shabbos* 33b).

7. "Ben Azzai, Ben Zoma, Ben Nannas" refers to Shimon ben Azzai, Shimon ben Zoma, and Shimon ben Nannas.

8. "Ben Beseira" refers to Rabbi Yehoshua ben Beseira.

9. "Ben Bag Bag" refers to Rabbi Yochanan ben Bag Bag.

10. "Yochanan Kohen Gadol" is the famous Yochanan ben Mattisyahu who is mentioned in our prayers when we give thanks for our victory over the Greek rulers.[*Al HaNissim* on Chanukah]

11. Rabbi Meir and Rabbi Nassan once wanted to embarrass Rabban Shimon, the father of Rabbi Yehudah HaNasi, (because of an incident that is too involved to be mentioned here). Thereupon, Rabban Gamliel denied them entry into his yeshivah (*Horayos* 13b). Therefore, when a *halachah* was quoted in the name of Rabbi Meir, they would quote it as "others say. . ," if it was quoted in Rabbi Nassan's name they would quote it as "some say . . ."

12. When Rabbi Yehudah HaNasi says in the Mishnah, "A certain disciple said before Rabbi Akiva, in the name of Rabbi Yishmael," that is *his* way of referring to Rabbi Meir (*Eiruvin* 13a).

13. "The learned ones said before the Sages . . ." refers to five scholars:
    Rabbi Shimon ben Azzai
    Rabbi Shimon ben Zoma
    Rabbi Shimon ben Nannas
    Chanan, and
    Chananiah Ish Ono.

14. Rabbi Meir is also called Rabbi Nehora'i. Both names have the same meaning (brilliant light). His original name was Rabbi Nechemiah.

15. When the Mishnah refers to *Chachamim*, "Sages", it sometimes is referring to one of the personalities we mentioned earlier, and sometimes it means the entire body of Sages; sometimes the *Gemara* explains who is meant by asking, "Who is meant by the term *"chachamim"*? And the *Gemara* will answer, "Rabbi so-and-so." This will happen if that particular Sage's opinion was accepted by many. Therefore, he is referred to as *chachamim*, although it was the opinion of only one individual.

16. When the Mishnah mentions *Beis Shammai* and *Beis Hillel*, [House of Shammai and House of Hillel] it refers to the group that followed Shammai's or Hillel's opinion, because a person's students are his household.

17. The title "Rebbi" refers to *Rabbeinu HaKadosh*, our holy teacher, Rabbi Yehudah HaNasi, the sixth in lineage after Hillel the Elder. He is the compiler of the Mishnah.

18. Wherever it says in the Mishnah, *"Be'emes ameru*—In truth they said . . ," it signifies *Halachah leMoshe miSinai*.

19. An anonymous Mishnah contains one of the following:

a. a derived law that the full body of Sages unanimously agreed on, or,

b. that which the full body of the Sages received from the Sages that came before it, as a law handed down generation after generation from Moshe. The last Sage in the line of transmission before Rabbi Yehudah HaNasi was Rabbi Meir, and that is what is meant by the phrase, "An anonymous Mishnah is by Rabbi Meir."

c. Some of the anonymous *mishnayos* may reflect Rabbi Meir's individual view, with which others disagree; or,

d. it may be by someone other than Rabbi Meir, whom the *Gemara* will identify.

When in my commentary, I will record the final halacha it will become clear which of the above alternatives is the case in each Mishnah.

Section Seven

The various titles the author of the Mishnah assigned to each of the Sages.

Rabbi Yehudah HaNasi classified the 128 Sages mentioned in the Mishnah into three categories. Those whom he ranked highest in eminence he simply called by their name. For example, he refers to Hillel and Shammai, to Shemaya and Avtalyon by their name and nothing else. He does this because of their towering greatness, since it was impossible to find a suitable title to express their magnificent stature, just as we give no accolades to the prophets.

Those Sages who, in his judgment, were below that level he gave the title "Rabban." For example, he speaks of *Rabban* Gamliel and *Rabban* Yochanan ben Zakkai.

Those who, in his opinion, were below this latter level, he gave the title "Rabbi," like *Rabbi* Meir and *Rabbi* Yehudah. He also called men on this level by the title *"Abba"* (Father), like *Abba* Shaul.

Sometimes he omits a title, without any particular reason, such as when he refers to Shimon Achi Azariah and Elazar Ish Bartosa.

Those personalities who are called simply by their names out of honor, and who therefore have no titles before their names are:

>Shimon HaTzaddik
>Antignos Ish Socho
>Yosi ben Yoezer
>Yosi ben Yochanan
>Yochanan Kohen Gadol
>Yehoshua ben Perachyah
>Nitai HaArbeili
>Choni HaMe'ageil
>Eliho'eini ben Hakaf
>Chanamel HaMitzri
>Yehudah ben Tabbai
>Shimon ben Shetach
>Sh'mayah
>Avtalyon
>Chanan
>Admon
>Akavya ben Mehalalel
>Hillel
>Shammai
>Nachum HaLavlar
>Chananiah ben Chizkiah ben Garon
>Bava ben Buta

Anyone mentioned in the Mishnah by his name alone, besides those in the above list, does have a title, but it has been omitted by Rabbi Yehudah HaNasi for no particular reason.

Section Eight

The various nicknames relating to country of origin, occupation, people and family.

The compiler of the Mishnah added various nicknames to the names of the transmitters of the Oral Law. Some of these have to do with their trade, such as Nachum HaLavlar, "the scribe," and Rabbi Shimon HaShezuri, "the spinner of threads."

Others he connected to their native lands, such as Ish Chadid, [the man from Chadid] Ish Ono and Ish Bartosa. The meaning of the nicknames Ish Tzereida [The personality of Tzereida], Ish Yerushalayim and other common places, is that he is the outstanding citizen of that place.

Others have their father's or brother's name added to their name, such as "This Rabbi ben [the son of] That Rabbi" or "This Rabbi achi [the brother of] That Rabbi." This happens very often. And some were identified by their family status, such a "So-and-so the Kohen."

APPENDIX

Section Nine

The Sages who were involved in most of the disputes in the Mishnah.

Those personalities who most often are involved in disputes in the Mishnah are:
Rabbi Meir
Rabbi Yehudah (ben Ila'i)
Rabbi Shimon (ben Yocha'i) and
Rabbi Yosi (ben Chalafta).

Controversies arise between any two in this group, and also among all four of them.

You will also find Rabbi Elazar disagreeing with any one of those four, but not as often as there are conflicts among these four.

The same is true for
Rabbi Akiva
Rabbi Eliezer and
Rabbi Yehoshua (ben Chanania)

You may find disputes between any two of them and among all three of them, but not as often as between the above mentioned four.

You will find disagreements also among
Rabbi Akiva
Rabbi Yishmael
Rabbi Tarfon and
Rabbi Elazar ben Azariah,
but fewer than among those mentioned above.

Fewer still, are the disputes between Beis Shammai and Beis Hillel.

Fewer yet, are the conflicts between Rabban Gamliel or Rabban Shimon ben Gamliel and Rebbi, and each one of the Sages mentioned above.

It is among these men that every dispute occurs in the majority of the Mishnah, with the exception of rare instances.

Section Ten

The number of times a Sage is mentioned in the Mishnah.

Some of the Sages who received the Oral Law have many laws quoted in their names, such as Rabbi Meir and Rabbi Yehudah. Others have only a few recorded in their names, e.g. Rabbi Elazar ben Yaakov, as the Sages said, "The Mishnah of Rabbi Eliezer ben Yaakov is small but good" (*Eiruvin* 62b), meaning his legal opinions are few in number but we accept his decisions.

The more often a person is involved in disputes, the more often his name will be quoted in the Mishnah.

Some of the Sages are mentioned only once in the Mishnah, and their names never occur again in connection with any legal matter.

There are thirty-seven such Sages:

1. Nachum HaLavlar and
2. Rabbi Miyasha are mentioned only in *maseches Pei'ah* (1:6), and their names never occur again elsewhere.

3. Chananiah ben Chachina'i and
4. Rabbi Yosef ben Hachotef Efrasi, in *Kilayim* (3:7 and 4:8) only.

5. Rabbi Elazar Chisma and
6. Rabbi Yosi ben Meshullam in *Terumos* (3:5; 4:8) only.

7. Rabbi Chutzpis in *Shevi'is* (10:6) only.

8. Rabbi Elazar ben Yehudah Ish Bartosa and
9. Dusta'i Ish K'far Demai, in *Orlah* (1:4; 2:5) only.

10. Nachum Hamadi in *Shabbos* (2:1) only.

11. Rabbi Ila'i and
12. Rabbi Dusta'i bar Rabbi Yannai, in (*Eiruvin* (2:6; 5:4) only.

APPENDIX

13. Rabbi Shimon ben HaSegan, and
14. ben Kovri, in *Shekalim* (1:4; 8:5) only.

15. Yehudah ben Tabbai
16. Shimon ben Shetach
17. Yosi ben Yoezer
18. Yosi ben Yochanan
19. Nitai HaArbeli and
20. Yehoshua ben Perachyah in *Chagigah* (2:2) only.

21. Shimon HaTeimani and
22. Nechemiah Ish Beis D'li, in *Yevamos* (4:13; 16:7) only.

23. Rabbi Elazar, son of Rabbi Yosi HaGelili and
24. Rabbi Yehoshua ben Hyrkanos in *Sotah* (5:3-5) only.

25. Yadua HaBavli in *Bava Metzia* (7:9) only.

26. Rabbi Shimon ben Yehudah in *Shavuos* (1:5) only.

27. Rabbi Shimon ben Beseira
28. Rabbi Nechuniah ben Elnasan Ish K'far HaBavli,
29. Rabbi Yosi HaKohen
30. Rabbi Yakim Ish Chadid and
31. Menachem ben Segana'i are mentioned in *Eiduyos* (6:2; 7:5-8; 8:1-2) only.

32. Shimon achi Azariah and
33. Yosi ben Choni in *Zevachim* (1:2) only.

34. Rabbi Elazar ben Rabbi Shimon in *Temurah* (4:4) only

35. Rabbi Yaakov in *Nega'im* (4:10), only.
36. Rabbi Elazar ben Pavi in *Tehoros* (7:9), only.

37. Rabbi Yochanan ben Yashua, son of Rabbi Akiva's father-in-law, in *Yadayim* (3:5), only.

All the Sages in this list have only one single halachah in the entire Mishnah quoted in their name, in the *masechta* we indicated.

This completes our Introduction to the Mishnah.

Glossary

ADAR – The twelfth Hebrew month
AGGADIC DERASHOS – Homiletic discourses
AL HANISSIM – The Prayer of thanksgiving recited on Chanukah
AMAH pl. *AMAS*: – cubit, cubits
ASMACHTA – mnemonic device

B'NEI YISRAEL – Children of Israel
BAMIDBAR – The Book of Numbers
BARAISA pl. *BARAISOS* – outside text, not included in the Mishnah
BEIS DIN – Jewish court
BEIS HAMIKDASH – Holy Temple
BEN – son of
BERACHAH pl. *BERACHOS*: – blessing
BEREISHIS – The Book of Genesis
BIRCHAS HAMAZONE – Grace after meals

CHALITZAH – the ceremony whereby a woman whose husband left no progeny is released from her obligation to marry her deceased husband's brother.

DERASH, DERASHAH – discourse
DEVARIM – The Book of Deuteronomy
DIVREI HAYAMIM – Chronicles

EIVER – a descendant of Noah
ELIYAHU – Elijah
ERETZ YISRAEL – The Land of Israel
ESROG – citron

GEMARA – Talmud
GEONIM – Sages who lived after the completion of the Talmud.
GEZEIRAH pl. *GEZEIROS* – protective measures
GITTIN – divorce

HALACHAH – law
HALACHAH LEMOSHE MISINAI – law handed down from Moses at Sinai
HASHEM – G-d

IYOV – Job

KARES – punishment of premature death
KESUVAH – marriage contract
KOHEIN pl. *KOHANIM*: – Priests, descendants of Aaron
KOHEIN GADOL – High Priest
KOHELES – Ecclesiastes

LEVI'IM – from the tribe of Levi
LULAV – palm branch take on Sukkos

MA'ASEROS – the tithes
MASECHES – Tractate of
MASECHTA pl. *MASECHTOS:* – Tractate
MELACHIM – The Book of Kings
MESUSHELACH – Methuselah
MEZUZAH – parchment scrolls containing the Shema that is placed on the doorpost.
MIKVEH – ritual immersion pool
MINHAGIM – customs
MISHLEI – Proverbs
MISHNAH pl. *MISHNAYOS*: – compilation of the oral tradition; it also refers to one paragraph of this compilation
MITZVAH pl. *MITZVOS*: – commandment

GLOSSARY

MOSHE RABBEINU – Moses our Teacher
MOUNT NEVO – Mount Nebo

NAZIR – nazirite—one who makes a vow to obstain from wine and from contact with the dead, he may also not cut his hair.
NIDDAH – menstruant woman

ORLAH – fruit of a tree within three years of its planting

PARASHAS – the portion [of the Torah]
PEREK – chapter
PRUZBUL – a document enabling one to collect his loans after the sh'mittah year

SEDER – order
SH'MITTAH – the sabbatical year when work in the field is prohibited
SHABBOS – The day of rest—Saturday
SHEM – son of Noah
SHEVAT – The eleventh Hebrew month
SHAVUOS – Festival of Weeks
SHEMOS – The Book of Exodus
SHIN – a letter of the Hebrew alphabet
SHIR HASHIRIM – Song of Songs
SHLOMOH – Solomon
SHMUEL – The Book of Samuel
SIDRAH – portion of the Torah
SUKKAH – hut used on Sukkos
SUKKOS – Festival of Tabernacles

TAHARAH – ritual purity
TAHOR – ritually pure
TAKKANOS – enactment
TAMEI – ritually impure
TEFILLIN – phylacteries
TEHILLIM – Psalms
TERUMAH – pl. *TERUMOS*: contribution to the Kohein
TOSEFTA – supplement
TUM'AH – ritual impurity

VAYIKRA – The Book of Leviticus

YAAKOV – Jacob
YECHEZKEL – Ezekiel
YEHOSHUA – Joshua
YERUSHALAYIM – Jerusalem
YESHAYAH – Isaiah
YIBBUM – levirate marriage where the wife of one who died without progeny, marries his brother.
YIRMIYAH – Jeremiah
YISRAEL – Israel
YOM TOV pl. *YAMIM TOVIM* – Festivals